Rethinking Language Education in the Digital Era

Digital Learning and the Future

Vol. 2

Series Editors:
Kieran McCartney (Open University) and
Graeme Davis (University of St Andrews)

Blanka Klímová, Marcel Pikhart, and Liqaa Habeb Al-Obaydi

Rethinking Language Education in the Digital Era

PETER LANG

Oxford · Berlin · Bruxelles · Chennai · Lausanne · New York

Bibliographic information published by the Deutsche Nationalbibliothek. The German National Library lists this publication in the German National Bibliography; detailed bibliographic data is available on the Internet at http://dnb.d-nb.de.

A catalogue record for this book is available from the British Library.
Library of Congress Control Number: 2025049352

Cover image: Liqaa Habeb Al-Obaydi, reproduced with permission.

ISSN 2634-8527
ISBN 978-1-80584-266-8 (Print)
ISBN 978-1-80584-267-5 (E-PDF)
ISBN 978-1-80584-268-2 (E-PUB)
DOI 10.3726/b23509

Published by Peter Lang Ltd, Oxford (United Kingdom)

info@peterlang.com

www.peterlang.com

Contents

Tables

Preface

Over the past two decades, foreign language education has been reshaped more radically than at any other time since the invention of the printing press. Cloud-based applications deliver adaptive drills to a learner's phone on the morning commute; large language models correct essays in seconds; virtual-reality head-sets place students in simulated markets, clinics and airports; and older adults meet with peers around the globe in moderated conversation circles that did not exist five years ago. What was once a field dominated by mimetic classroom routines and carefully sequenced textbooks has become an ecosystem of apps, platforms and data *pipelines* whose scale, speed and sociocultural reach are unprecedented. Rethinking Language Education in the Digital Era: A New Linguistic Landscape responds to this watershed moment. Bringing together scholars working at the intersections of applied linguistics, educational tech-nology, cognitive psychology and ethics, the monograph offers a panoramic yet critically balanced account of how digital tools are redefining what it means to teach and to learn another language.

Although computers entered the language classroom in the late 1970s, their role remained peripheral for decades: word-processing, multimedia CD-ROMs, the occasional chat room. By contrast, today's learners inhabit a digital civilisa-tion in which language practices, texting, streaming, posting, translating, are inseparable from the infrastructures that support them. Chapter 1 therefore opens with a cartography of 'latest trends in digital foreign language educa-tion'. It traces the migration from desktop CALL to mobile-assisted language learning (MALL); the rise of AI-powered chatbots that deliver form-focused feedback in real time; and the growing importance of immersive, multimodal environments such as augmented-reality cultural walks and serious games. By anchoring the discussion in empirical studies published between 2020 and 2025, the chapter establishes a contemporary baseline against which the remainder of the volume builds.

Digital innovations do not reach learners in a vacuum. Access, motivation and perceived usefulness vary markedly across age cohorts. In Chapter 2 the authors adopt a lifespan perspective, contrasting the habits of 'digital natives' – university students who fluidly combine Duolingo streaks with TikTok syntax hacks – with those of 'digital newcomers', older adults who may value cognitive maintenance or cultural enrichment over test scores. This comparative lens is especially timely: by 2050, one in six people worldwide will be over sixty-five, yet gerontological design principles are rarely considered in mainstream language apps. The chapter synthesises survey data, usability studies and ethnographic vignettes to show how scaffolding, interface simplicity and opportunities for social bonding can bridge generational divides, yielding more inclusive digital curricula.

Digitalisation promises efficiency, but at what cognitive cost – or benefit? Chapter 3 reviews research on cognitive gain in digital language learning, parsing a growing but still fragmented literature that links technologically mediated practice to enhancements in memory, executive function and mental flexibility. Meta-analyses suggest that spaced repetition algorithms and multimodal encoding confer measurable advantages, yet other studies warn of superficial processing and split attention. By juxtaposing findings from neurolinguistics, behavioural psychology and classroom experimentation, the authors formulate a research agenda that replaces techno-determinism with nuanced, evidence-based inquiry.

Games are no longer peripheral playthings; they are sophisticated engines of narrative, collaboration and feedback. Chapter 4 dissects the pedagogical logic of digital game-mediated language learning. It distinguishes educational games, commercial off-the-shelf titles and 'serious' simulations, mapping each to relevant motivational and sociocultural theories. Crucially, the chapter does not idealise gamification; it scrutinises cognitive load, equity of access, and the risk of privileging short-term engagement metrics over durable proficiency. Case studies from Europe, Asia and Latin America illustrate how thoughtfully integrated gaming can amplify speaking fluency, pragmatic awareness and intercultural empathy when aligned with clear instructional outcomes.

If the first four chapters chart possibilities, Chapter 5 sounds a note of caution. The ethical considerations surrounding data capture, algorithmic bias, intellectual property and digital well-being are examined in depth. The authors argue that language educators occupy a dual role as facilitators of communication and stewards of learners' rights. They unpack scenarios in which automated writing assistants may blur authorship, where predictive analytics could reinforce linguistic hegemonies, and where the 'attention economy' undermines sustained reflection. The chapter proposes actionable guidelines – transparent consent protocols, bias audits, and curricula that foster AI literacy – to ensure that innovation remains accountable to diverse learner populations.

The closing substantive chapter confronts the accelerating trajectory of generative AI. Tools such as ChatGPT, Copilot, Gemini or DeepSeek are analysed not only for their technical affordances – multilingual text generation, conversational tutoring, multimodal search, but also for their socio-educational ramifications. Through thematic analysis of recent pilot studies, the authors show how AI can augment formative assessment, differentiate instruction and scaffold creativity. Yet they also foreground unresolved dilemmas: hallucination, privacy, environmental cost. The chapter culminates in a future vision that balances adaptive intelligence with human-centred pedagogy, recommending hybrid models in which educators orchestrate, rather than outsource, the learning process.

To facilitate navigation, each chapter follows a common architecture:

- Introduction: situates the focal theme historically and conceptually.
- State of the art: synthesises empirical findings published since 2015.
- Critical issues: interrogates assumptions, gaps and contradictions.
- Pedagogical implications: translates theory into actionable strategies.
- Future directions: outlines emerging questions for the next research cycle.

Overall, although the monograph is grounded in scholarly rigour, it is written with a wide readership in mind. Researchers can find comprehensive literature reviews and agendas for future enquiry. Teacher educators and instructional designers might gain design heuristics for MOOCs, blended courses and mobile apps. Policymakers concerned with digital inclusion, lifelong learning and AI governance can discover evidence-based recommendations. Finally, practitioners may encounter contextualised examples that can be adapted to local constraints and opportunities.

In an era when a single click can summon instant translation or generate a personalised grammar drill, it is tempting to view technology as either panacea or peril. *Rethinking Language Education in the Digital Era* refuses this binary. Instead, it shows that the educational value of digital tools emerges at the intersection of design, pedagogy, ethics and context. By foregrounding human agency – of learners, teachers, designers and policymakers – the monograph argues that digitalisation is not an external force acting upon language education but a terrain negotiated through mindful choices.

Abbreviations

AI	Artificial Intelligence
AR	Augmented Reality
CEFR	Common European Framework of Reference for Languages
EFL	English as a Foreign Language
ESL	English as a Second Language
FERPA	Family Educational Rights and Privacy Act
FLE	Foreign Language Education
FLL	Foreign Language Learning
GDPR	General Data Protection Regulation
IDLE	Informal Digital Learning of English
L2	Second Language
LMS	Learning Management System
MALL	Mobile-Assisted Language Learning
NLP	Natural Language Processing
NMT	Neural Machine Translation
NUI	Natural User Interface
RAG	Retrieval-Augmented Generation
SDL	Self-Directed Learning
STEM	Science, Technology, Engineering and Mathematics disciplines
TAM	Technology Acceptance Model
TOEIC	Test of English for International Communication
UX	User Experience
VR	Virtual Reality

CHAPTER 1

Latest trends in digital foreign language education

The landscape of foreign language education has undergone a significant transformation in recent years, driven by rapid advancements in digital technology. Traditional classroom-based methods are increasingly being supplemented or replaced by innovative digital tools and platforms, making language learning more accessible, personalised, and engaging. Digital technologies are transforming the landscape of foreign language education (FLE), fostering new methods of instruction, expanding access, and reshaping how learners engage with content across generations (Şişianu & Puşcaşu, 2024). Recent advances, particularly in AI, mobile learning, and virtual reality, are enhancing both the delivery and the effectiveness of foreign language learning (FLL) (Nicolaidou, Pissas, & Boglou, 2021). These changes are not only impacting younger generations of digital natives but are also increasingly embraced by older adults, who seek to improve cognitive function, social engagement, and lifelong learning prospects through digital FLL (Chu et al., 2022; Klimova, 2020). As the world becomes increasingly interconnected and reliant on digital communication, the demand for effective language acquisition methods has risen. Technologies, such as mobile applications, chatbots, machine translation, and AI-driven personalised learning platforms have emerged as dominant tools in this evolving landscape (Ali, 2020; Jiang, 2022). These tools offer flexibility, motivation, and adaptive support to diverse learner groups, ranging from university students to retired adults. While many of these tools are widely known, their implementation in various demographic contexts, especially among older learners, remains under-researched (Iskakova, 2024). Traditional approaches are giving way to learner-centred models empowered by technology, yet the pedagogical frameworks and accessibility considerations vary significantly across age groups (Wang, 2023).

FLL has historically evolved alongside advancements in communication technologies. From audio-lingual labs in the mid-twentieth century to multimedia software in the 1990s and online platforms in the 2000s, each wave of innovation has brought new tools and pedagogies. In the last two decades, the growth of internet access and mobile technologies has allowed for real-time, location-independent language instruction (Jia et al., 2022). This evolution has been particularly accelerated by the advent of artificial intelligence (AI) and machine learning, which offer tailored feedback, adaptive learning paths, and natural language interaction capabilities (Gligorea et al., 2023). Mobile-assisted language learning (MALL) has revolutionised FLE by offering ubiquitous and flexible access to learning materials. Applications, such as Duolingo, Babbel, and Rosetta Stone have attracted millions of users by gamifying the learning process and offering bite-sized lessons (Karasimos, 2022; Meltzer et al., 2021). These platforms also use spaced repetition systems, voice recognition, and reward-based mechanics to maintain learner engagement (Godsk & Møller, 2025).

AI-powered chatbots and virtual tutors represent another significant leap. They simulate human conversation and provide immediate corrective feedback, enabling real-time practice and immersive experiences (Adamopoulou & Moussiades, 2020). In addition, tools like ChatGPT are now being explored as interactive writing assistants and conversational partners, offering grammar correction, translation, and content generation services (Johnston et al., 2024; Thelwall, 2024). Neural machine translation (NMT) tools, such as Google Translate and DeepL, are also playing a growing role in language education. Though traditionally used as auxiliary tools, recent studies highlight their potential for improving vocabulary acquisition and reading comprehension when integrated effectively into classroom practice (Klimova et al., 2022; Urlaub & Dessein, 2022).

Despite these advancements, there are persistent concerns regarding the quality of automated feedback, the depth of cultural immersion, and ethical issues surrounding data privacy and over-reliance on automation. Moreover, disparities in digital access and digital literacy levels may hinder the full integration of these tools, particularly among older adults or underserved populations. The COVID-19 pandemic further accelerated the digital transformation of FLE, forcing institutions to adopt online tools and prompting learners of all ages to explore virtual options. This disruption highlighted both the resilience and the limitations of digital FLL systems, reinforcing the need for inclusive, adaptable, and pedagogically sound approaches (Fong et al., 2022; Klimova & Pikhart, 2022).

Emerging AI-based tools in FLE

AI has become one of the most transformative forces in FLE, offering tools that not only enhance instruction but also personalise the learning experience. AI-driven applications provide learners with instant feedback, simulate human-like interactions, and adapt dynamically to individual learner progress (Joshi, 2024). These tools support diverse learning objectives, from vocabulary acquisition to pronunciation training, and have been increasingly integrated into both formal and informal learning contexts (Ali, 2020; Jiang, 2022).

One of the most impactful applications of AI in FLL is the use of chatbots. These AI-powered conversational agents simulate human dialogue and are capable of providing real-time responses in the target language. Tools like Replika, HelloTalk, and Mondly's chatbot function as virtual interlocutors, offering a safe environment for learners to practice without the anxiety that often accompanies live interaction (Adamopoulou & Moussiades, 2020; Du & Alm, 2024). Chatbots are particularly useful in developing communicative competence, as they can correct grammatical errors, suggest appropriate vocabulary, and prompt more natural language production (Şahin Kızıl, Klimova, Pikhart, & Parmaxi, 2025). Although they are still limited in contextual nuance and emotional depth, recent iterations have shown substantial improvements, enabling users to engage in increasingly complex conversations (Xiao, Zhang, & He, 2024). The emergence of ChatGPT has pushed the boundaries of chatbot interaction even further by allowing more fluid, personalised exchanges and offering learners the ability to explore topics of interest in their target language (Johnston et al., 2024).

Smartphone applications powered by AI are now a staple of FLL. Duolingo, for instance, integrates AI algorithms to tailor the difficulty and pacing of lessons to individual users, while also incorporating gamification to maintain motivation (Meltzer et al., 2021). Apps, such as Babbel and Rosetta Stone also use machine learning to track learner performance and provide targeted review exercises (Essafi, Belfakir, & Moubtassime, 2024). These platforms offer a blend of repetition, listening practice, and voice-based interaction, which are ideal for self-paced learning environments. For older learners, custom apps such as SprachenTanz and Senioreng have emerged, focusing on cognitive stimulation, ease of navigation, and social interaction features (Puebla et al., 2022). These tools are often co-designed with educators and end-users, ensuring age-appropriate content and accessibility.

In addition, NMT tools, such as Google Translate and DeepL, use deep learning to produce more accurate and context-sensitive translations than their rule-based predecessors. While NMT was initially intended for practical communication, it has increasingly been incorporated into the language learning process. Learners now use these tools to explore sentence structure, vocabulary, and syntax by comparing machine translations with native usage (Klimova et al., 2022; Urlaub & Dessein, 2022). Furthermore, AI-powered writing assistants, such as Grammarly and QuillBot are also becoming integral to language learning, especially for academic and professional contexts. These tools offer real-time feedback on grammar, style, tone, and coherence, encouraging learners to reflect critically on their written output and revise accordingly (Singh et al., 2023).

Technologies, such as Amazon Alexa, Google Assistant, and Apple's Siri are now capable of supporting language learning through spoken interaction (Leblebici, 2024). These devices can be programmed to answer questions, define vocabulary, or conduct simple conversations in multiple languages. Their speech recognition capabilities are particularly beneficial for pronunciation training, as they help users detect and correct mispronunciations in real time (Shandilya & Fan, 2022). This functionality is particularly valuable for older learners, who may benefit from repetitive oral practice to reinforce cognitive and linguistic retention. Studies have found that speech-based interaction with AI can improve learners' confidence and willingness to speak in a foreign language (Wang & Christiansen, 2019).

AI-driven platforms, for example Lingvist and Elsa Speak use predictive analytics to adapt instruction based on learner behaviour and performance. These platforms personalise content delivery, monitor progress, and offer targeted exercises to address individual weaknesses (Tiwari et al., 2024). Adaptive systems can detect patterns in learner errors, provide scaffolded support, and adjust instructional pathways to maintain an optimal level of challenge and engagement (Jia et al., 2022). In addition to traditional language skills, some platforms are beginning to incorporate intercultural competence training, helping learners understand not just linguistic structures but also the sociocultural context of communication. This trend aligns with broader educational goals outlined by the Common European Framework of Reference for Languages (CEFR, 2020).

AI is also being used to automate content creation and assessment. Teachers can now use tools like ChatGPT to generate quizzes, dialogue simulations, and reading comprehension exercises tailored to specific learner levels. In assessment, AI tools are being developed to provide formative feedback on oral and written performance, freeing instructors to focus on more complex pedagogical tasks (Ghafar et al., 2023). However, concerns remain about the reliability and fairness of AI-generated assessments, especially regarding bias and the potential for misinterpretation of nuanced language. As AI becomes more embedded in assessment practices, the need for ethical oversight and human moderation becomes paramount (Klimova, Pikhart, & Kacetl, 2023).

Pedagogical implications of emerging technologies in FLE

As Klimova and Pikhart (2025) claim, the rapid integration of digital tools, especially those powered by AI, has redefined pedagogical strategies in FLL. These technologies offer new opportunities for personalised learning, increased learner autonomy, and multimodal interaction. At the same time, they challenge educators to rethink traditional roles, design inclusive curricula, and develop ethical frameworks for digital use. Pedagogical implications vary across learner demographics but share common threads that shape contemporary FLL practices. Emerging technologies have accelerated the shift from teacher-centred approaches to learner-centred models. AI-powered tools such as ChatGPT, Duolingo, and Rosetta Stone enable learners to control the pace, content, and method of their language acquisition (Mai, Da, & Hanh, 2024). This autonomy is particularly beneficial in self-directed and lifelong learning contexts, where learners may engage with content outside of formal classrooms. For educators, this shift means transitioning from knowledge transmitters to facilitators, curators, and learning designers. Teachers must help students navigate the abundance of online tools and select those that align with their linguistic goals, cognitive styles, and technical skills (Klimova & Pikhart, 2022). In the case of older adults, this includes guiding them through onboarding processes and ensuring that they are not overwhelmed by technology.

AI enables personalised instruction that can adapt to individual learners' progress and needs. Adaptive platforms like Lingvist, Elsa Speak, and Duolingo use learner data to adjust difficulty levels, provide targeted feedback, and suggest review materials (Jia et al., 2022). This approach can significantly improve learning outcomes by maintaining the learner's optimal zone of development. Pedagogically, personalisation requires teachers to understand how these systems work and how to integrate them effectively into syllabi (Lasmawan, & Budiarta, 2020). While adaptive tools can handle repetitive tasks and progress tracking, educators must ensure that personalisation does not compromise communicative competence or intercultural understanding. For instance, automated grammar correction should be paired with authentic communicative tasks to reinforce functional language use (Ali, 2020).

Emerging technologies have made FLL more multimodal, engaging learners through text, audio, video, interactive dialogue, and gamification. Multimodal learning addresses different sensory modalities and learning preferences, helping students reinforce linguistic structures and meanings across contexts (Ghafar et al., 2023). In practice, this means designing language tasks that combine various input and output channels. For example, a learning module may include listening to a native speaker podcast (auditory), answering chatbot questions (interactive), and recording spoken reflections (productive). Educators should also consider asynchronous and mobile-friendly formats to support ubiquitous learning, particularly for adult learners balancing study with other life responsibilities (Fong et al., 2022). Therefore, gamification is a common strategy included in many FLL tools (Al-Obaydi et al., 2025). Features, such as progress bars, achievement badges, and leaderboards motivate learners by tapping into competitive and reward-based behaviours. Duolingo's streak tracking and point systems have been widely cited as effective for maintaining user engagement (Karasimos, 2022; Meltzer et al., 2021). Feedback, too, plays a critical pedagogical role. AI systems offer immediate feedback on grammar, pronunciation, and vocabulary use. However, it is often limited to surface-level corrections. Teachers must supplement automated feedback with human insight that addresses pragmatic, sociocultural, and contextual aspects of communication (Klimova & Pikhart, 2022). In the case of older learners, positive reinforcement and low-stress environments are key for sustaining engagement and confidence (Schiller, Dorner, & Szabó, 2023).

While many AI tools are designed for individual use, the value of collaborative learning remains high. Digital platforms that incorporate social features, such as group chats, peer assessments, or tandem partnerships, can promote interaction and intercultural exchange (Kim et al., 2025). Research (Puebla et al., 2022; Wang & Christiansen, 2019) shows that social components are particularly beneficial for older learners, who value communication and connection as part of the learning process. Educators should intentionally design collaborative tasks that use technology as a bridge rather than a barrier to social interaction. Examples include co-authoring digital stories, participating in online language forums, or using shared virtual whiteboards for brainstorming in the target language. For instance, Teng (2021) in his study investigated how interactive whiteboard technology influences collaborative writing among EFL students by examining their writing achievement, metacognitive activities, and co-regulation patterns during group writing tasks.

The increased reliance on AI in FLL necessitates a strong emphasis on ethical and digital literacy. Learners must be taught not only how to use these tools but also how to use them responsibly. This includes understanding AI limitations, recognising misinformation, citing AI-generated content, and respecting data privacy (Alrayes, Henari, & Ahmed, 2024; Thelwall, 2024). Pedagogically, this calls for integration of critical thinking and media literacy into language curricula. Vieriu and Petrea (2025) in their study emphasise that educators should encourage learners to question the sources of content, evaluate the credibility of translations or answers, and reflect on the role of AI in shaping language norms and values. As Klimova, Pikhart, and Kacetl (2023) argue, ethical training must be included not just in student learning, but in the design of AI-powered educational systems.

For technology integration to be successful, educators themselves need support. Many instructors feel unprepared to implement AI tools effectively and ethically in their teaching (Lee et al., 2024). Professional development programmes must address both the technical aspects of using AI tools and the pedagogical shifts required for their meaningful integration. Workshops, communities of practice, and collaborative pilot projects can help educators experiment with tools, exchange ideas, and develop best practices. Furthermore, institutions should encourage interdisciplinary cooperation between language educators, instructional designers, and AI developers to ensure that emerging technologies align with pedagogical goals.

Challenges and limitations of digital FLL tools

However, research studies (Klimova, Pikhart & Kacetl, 2023; Nguyen, Lai, & Nguyen, 2024) indicate that despite the transformative potential of digital technologies in FLL, their implementation is not without challenges. These limitations span technical, pedagogical, psychological, ethical, and institutional dimensions. Recognising and addressing these issues is essential to maximising the educational value of emerging tools while minimising their drawbacks, especially in increasingly diverse learner populations.

One of the most persistent barriers to effective digital FLL is unequal access to technology and digital literacy. While many younger learners are adept at using digital tools, older adults, marginalised populations, and learners from low-income backgrounds may lack the skills, confidence, or resources to fully benefit from these innovations (Faverio, 2022; Klimova & Sanda, 2021). Limited internet connectivity, outdated devices, or lack of training can result in fragmented learning experiences and increased frustration. These digital divides can further exacerbate educational inequality unless counterbalanced by inclusive design, outreach programmes, and institutional support (Sixsmith et al., 2022). While AI-driven platforms often aim to simplify learning, the sheer volume of digital content, notifications, and multitasking demands can lead to cognitive overload, particularly among older users or learners with attention difficulties. Complex interfaces or poorly structured content can overwhelm users, leading to reduced motivation and disengagement (Shandilya & Fan, 2022). Gamified applications, while motivating, may also encourage short-term engagement at the expense of deep learning (Al-Obaydi et al., 2025). Learners may focus on earning points or completing streaks rather than mastering linguistic competence (Karasimos,

2022). Educators must ensure that technology use is balanced, purposeful, and cognitively sustainable.

One of the more pressing pedagogical concerns is the risk of superficial learning (Mogavi, et al., 2024). Tools like machine translation, grammar checkers, and chatbots may enable learners to bypass deep cognitive engagement with language structures. Over-reliance on AI-generated responses can diminish critical thinking, creativity, and problem-solving skills – abilities essential for real-world language use (Ahadzadeh, Wu, & Sijia, 2024; Pavlenko & Syzenko, 2024). Studies (Vieriu & Petrea, 2025; Zhai, Wibowo, & Li, 2024) show that students often accept AI outputs without verifying accuracy or understanding underlying principles. This issue is compounded by the 'black box' nature of many AI systems, where the logic behind feedback or suggestions remains opaque to the user (Singh et al., 2023). Educators need to scaffold AI use with metacognitive strategies that prompt learners to reflect, evaluate, and question.

Furthermore, the ethical use of AI in FLL presents a growing area of concern. Many platforms collect and analyse personal data to provide personalised feedback, raising questions about consent, data ownership, and surveillance (Klimova, Pikhart, & Kacetl, 2023). Older adults in particular may be unaware of privacy risks, underscoring the need for transparent policies and user-friendly consent mechanisms. Bias in AI algorithms is another issue. Language models are trained on vast datasets that may reflect stereotypes or inaccuracies. If not properly moderated, these biases can influence learners' perceptions of language and culture (Du & Alm, 2024). Plagiarism is also a concern, especially in academic contexts. Students may submit AI-generated writing without proper attribution or critical engagement. As surveys indicate, many students fail to cite ChatGPT use in their assignments despite being aware of institutional guidelines (Pallivathukal et al., 2024). Institutions must therefore establish clear policies for acceptable AI use, along with educational programmes that emphasise academic integrity.

Although many digital tools are readily available, their integration into formal curricula often lags behind. Teachers may feel unprepared, lack institutional support, or be unsure how to align technology use with learning outcomes (Lee et al., 2024). Some instructors are hesitant to adopt AI tools due to concerns about pedagogical validity, loss of control, or job displacement (Gomathi, 2024). Without proper integration, digital tools may become isolated add-ons rather than enriching components of the language learning ecosystem. Suman and Suman (2023) state that effective use requires alignment between tools, pedagogy, and assessment, supported by ongoing training and evaluation.

Many commercial FLL applications are designed for a general audience, with limited flexibility in content adaptation (Ali et al., 2025). Lessons may be overly simplistic, irrelevant to adult learners, or culturally insensitive. Older learners, in particular, often seek content that reflects their real-life experiences, interests, and values (Puebla et al., 2022; van der Ploeg, Keijzer, & Lowie, 2023). Moreover, cultural nuances are often underrepresented in AI-generated content. Tools may focus on grammatical correctness or vocabulary frequency without addressing idiomatic expressions, pragmatics, or intercultural competence. This undermines the holistic nature of language education and limits learners' ability to function in authentic communicative contexts (CEFR, 2020).

Although the use of AI in FLL is expanding, empirical research remains limited, especially regarding its long-term effectiveness and impact on diverse learner populations. Most studies are exploratory, short-term, or focused on higher education settings. There is a lack of controlled studies, longitudinal data, and comparative analyses between AI-supported and traditional instruction (Klimova et al., 2023; Nijmeijer et al., 2021). In addition, there is no unified framework for evaluating the pedagogical value of AI tools. As Al-Huwail et al. (2025) maintain, most assessments focus on usability or learner satisfaction, while neglecting deeper measures such as communicative competence, intercultural understanding, or language retention. Addressing this research gap is essential for evidence-based policy and practice.

Future directions and recommendations

As digital technologies continue to evolve, their role in FLL is expected to deepen and diversify. To ensure that these tools are pedagogically effective, ethically sound, and universally accessible, future efforts must focus on innovation, inclusivity, and sustainability. For older adults, this involves addressing sensory limitations, simplifying user interfaces, and integrating training modules or tutorials. Developers should collaborate with gerontologists, educators, and end-users to co-design applications that align with older learners' cognitive styles, social preferences, and content relevance (Puebla et al., 2022; Klimova & Sanda, 2021). In parallel, youth-oriented tools should support critical digital literacy and reflection, helping learners understand when and how to use AI-generated content effectively. Offering adjustable features, for example, simplified vs. advanced modes, can accommodate learners of differing experience and comfort levels. To enrich digital FLL experiences, future models should incorporate interdisciplinary perspectives from fields such as cognitive science, education, linguistics, computer science, and human–computer interaction. This will ensure a more holistic understanding of how learners interact with technology and how AI can support not just linguistic accuracy but broader communicative and cultural competencies (Chu et al., 2022; Zhang, 2023).

Likewise, intergenerational learning models, where older and younger learners collaborate through technology, can promote mutual digital literacy, cross-generational empathy, and motivation. Projects that pair younger digital natives with older learners as peer tutors or partners in language exchange are promising for community building and knowledge-sharing.

The traditional foreign language curriculum must be reimagined to accommodate the possibilities of AI and digital tools. This includes rethinking instructional design, formative assessment, and teacher roles. As Wlater (2024) suggest, future pedagogies should:

- include AI-assisted writing, speaking, and translation tasks within course syllabi,
- incorporate modules on ethical AI use, critical thinking, and media literacy,
- promote project-based and inquiry-driven learning using real-world digital tools,
- encourage collaborative learning environments supported by AI tutors and forums.

Educators will need professional development to confidently integrate these tools, and institutions must invest in capacity-building initiatives that include training, mentorship, and cross-departmental collaboration (Lee et al., 2024).

AI has the potential to revolutionise assessment by offering real-time, personalised feedback. However, future systems must move beyond simple grammar correction to include feedback on fluency, coherence, cultural appropriateness, and communicative effectiveness. This requires more sophisticated natural language processing models and careful calibration by educators to avoid over-standardisation (Ali, 2020; Thelwall, 2024). Furthermore, AI-generated assessment should complement – rather than replace – human evaluation. Teachers play a critical role in interpreting learner performance, identifying growth areas, and fostering motivation. Hybrid assessment models that combine automated diagnostics with teacher guidance offer the most balanced path forward.

As AI tools become more embedded in education, comprehensive ethical frameworks are urgently needed. Future policies should address:

- informed consent and transparency in how user data is collected, stored, and used,
- bias auditing to detect and mitigate linguistic, cultural, or demographic biases in AI models,

- academic integrity policies outlining acceptable use of AI for assignments and evaluations,
- privacy standards compliant with global data protection laws (e.g. GDPR, FERPA).

Educational institutions should establish ethics committees, involve students in policy discussions, and offer regular workshops on responsible AI use (Klimova, Pikhart, & Kacetl, 2023; Alrayes, Henari, & Ahmed, 2024).

More rigorous, large-scale research is needed to determine the long-term impact of digital and AI tools on FLL outcomes. Future studies should:

- use longitudinal and comparative designs to evaluate learning effectiveness,
- explore underrepresented groups, such as older adults, refugees, or learners with disabilities,
- examine the role of affective factors, such as motivation, anxiety, and identity, in digital learning,
- investigate how language acquisition differs across tools, contexts, and learner profiles.

Standardised metrics and cross-institutional research collaborations can help build a more cohesive body of evidence that informs educational policy and technological innovation (Klimova et al., 2023; Nijmeijer et al., 2021).

Finally, the future of digital FLL depends on collaboration across borders, sectors, and disciplines. International consortia, government programmes, and NGOs should support initiatives that:

- promote open-access FLL tools in underserved regions,
- translate and localise content to preserve linguistic diversity,
- encourage cross-cultural exchanges via digital platforms,
- fund pilot projects for emerging technologies like VR/AR and AI tutors.

This global approach will help democratise access to quality language education and ensure that no learner, regardless of age, background, or location, is left behind in the digital era.

CHAPTER 2

Use of digital technologies among young and older adults

As stated in the previous chapter, the increasing presence of digital technologies in education has transformed the landscape of FLE, offering learners of all ages new opportunities for interaction, self-direction, and personalised learning (Bećirović, Brdarević-Čeljo, & Delić, 2021). From mobile applications, such as Duolingo and Babbel to AI-powered chatbots and neural machine translation systems, learners are now able to access immersive language environments beyond the traditional classroom setting (Adamopoulou & Moussiades, 2020; Klimova et al., 2023). This transformation is particularly significant in an era marked by global mobility, demographic aging, and technological innovation.

Traditionally, the adoption of digital tools in education has been closely associated with younger adults, often referred to as *digital natives* (Prensky, 2001). Their familiarity with technology from an early age allows them to engage fluently with a wide range of applications and platforms, using them for both formal and informal language learning. Recent research (Du & Alm, 2024; Kavadella et al., 2024) confirms that university students increasingly use AI tools, such as ChatGPT for brainstorming, writing assistance, and comprehension of complex academic texts. These tools enhance academic performance, motivation, and language proficiency when integrated responsibly (Hasanein & Sobaih, 2023). However, there is also growing interest in understanding how older adults engage with similar technologies. As populations age and life expectancy increases, lifelong learning becomes a crucial strategy for maintaining cognitive health, social participation, and personal fulfilment (Narushima, Liu, & Diestelkamp, 2018). Foreign language learning offers a particularly rich domain for such engagement, as it stimulates cognitive function, enhances social connection, and supports intercultural understanding (Klimova, 2020; Schiller, Dorner, & Szabó, 2023). Recent studies (Fang, Liu, & Peng, 2024; Pihlainen et al., 2022; Puebla et al., 2022) reveal that older adults are willing to experiment with digital tools for language learning, especially when such tools are adapted to their needs and supported by user-friendly design and social interaction opportunities.

Despite the promising developments, important gaps remain in our understanding of how different age groups interact with emerging language technologies. While younger users may seek speed, efficiency, and gamification, older learners often value clarity, cognitive stimulation, and the social aspects of learning (Wulan et al., 2024). These generational differences highlight the need for a nuanced understanding of pedagogical design, accessibility, and ethical considerations in digital language education (Klimova & Sanda, 2021; Reiss, 2021).

The integration of digital technologies into FLE is supported by several theoretical perspectives that explain the role of technology in learning, as well as the cognitive, motivational, and social factors that influence learner engagement across age groups. For instance, Vygotsky's sociocultural theory emphasises the role of social interaction and cultural tools in cognitive development. Language, as both a cognitive and social tool, is learned more effectively in interaction with others and through the use of mediating artefacts (Vygotsky, 1978). In digital contexts, technologies, such as chatbots, video conferencing platforms, and collaborative apps act as mediating tools that support communication and scaffold learners' development. This theory is particularly relevant for older adults, who benefit from socially meaningful learning environments that support autonomy, reduce isolation, and foster a sense of community (Puebla et al., 2022). For younger learners, digital platforms offer opportunities for peer interaction, co-construction of meaning, and immediate feedback, key components in promoting language acquisition (Iglesias-Diéguez, Martínez-Adrián, & Gallardo-del-Puerto, 2025). The communicative and collaborative affordances of technologies are associated with sociocultural principles, especially when learners are encouraged to engage in authentic, purposeful communication (Su, & Zou, 2020).

Another is the concept of lifelong learning which is crucial in the context of older adult education. Lifelong learning refers to the continuous development of skills and knowledge throughout an individual's life. In aging societies, language learning is increasingly viewed as a form of cognitive enrichment and social engagement that contributes to active aging and improved quality of life (Klimova, 2020). Research (Grossmann et al., 2023; Meltzer et al., 2021) indicates that language learning can enhance memory, attention, and executive functioning in older adults, thereby delaying cognitive decline. Digital tools support lifelong learning by offering flexible, personalised, and accessible learning opportunities. However, for older learners to fully benefit from these technologies, they must be designed with age-related changes in cognition, vision, hearing, and motor skills in mind (Chu et al., 2022). Moreover, effective learning requires not only access to technology but also digital literacy and pedagogical support (Klimova & Sanda, 2021).

Furthermore, the concept of digital literacy plays an important role in FLE. It refers to the ability to access, evaluate, create, and communicate information using digital technologies. This skill set varies significantly between generations. Younger adults, often labelled *digital natives*, are generally more comfortable navigating digital environments, although this does not always translate into critical digital literacy (Bouzar, El Idrissi, & Ghourdou, 2024; Prensky, 2001). Their use of digital tools tends to be frequent and exploratory, with a strong preference for tools that offer immediate, gamified, and user-centred experiences (Karasimos, 2022). In contrast, older adults, often considered *digital immigrants*, may experience greater barriers to technology adoption, including anxiety, lack of confidence, or physical limitations (Zhang, 2023). However, studies (Faverio, 2022; Shandilya & Fan, 2022) increasingly show that these barriers can be overcome with appropriate training, user-friendly design, and clear perceived benefits. Older learners who engage in technology-supported FLE often do so for intrinsic motivations, such as cognitive stimulation, personal fulfilment, and social connection (Puebla et al., 2021; Wang & Christiansen, 2019).

Also, motivation plays a central role in technology-assisted language learning (Stockwell, 2013). For both age groups, intrinsic and extrinsic motivational factors shape engagement. Young adults are often motivated by academic achievement, employability, and social recognition, while older adults may be driven by personal interest, cultural curiosity, or the desire to maintain cognitive health (Klimova, 2020; Schiller, Dorner, & Szabó, 2023).

Self-directed learning (SDL) is another key concept, especially relevant in digital contexts where learners must often set their own goals, manage time, and assess progress. Mobile apps, AI-powered platforms, and learning management systems (LMS) can support SDL by offering structured content, adaptive feedback, and progress tracking (Klimova & Pikhart, 2022). However, successful self-directed learning depends on digital confidence and familiarity, which tend to be higher in younger learners but can be developed in older adults through targeted support (Sanda & Klimova, 2021).

Digital technologies in FLE and young adults

The use of digital technologies in FLE has expanded rapidly in recent years, providing both young and older learners with a wide range of tools to support language acquisition (Gu, 2024). These tools range from mobile applications and language learning platforms to artificial intelligence (AI)-powered assistants, chatbots, and immersive virtual environments. However, the nature of engagement with these technologies varies considerably across age groups due to differences in digital literacy, learning goals, cognitive preferences, and social contexts (Campos, & Scherer, 2024).

Young adults, particularly university students, have been quick to adopt digital technologies in their foreign language learning journeys. Their familiarity with smartphones, social media, and internet-based tools has made them highly receptive to integrating educational technologies into both formal and informal learning contexts (Singh, Tayarani-Najaran, & Yaqoob, 2023). Digital platforms provide this demographic with flexibility, autonomy, and gamified experiences that align well with their fast-paced and multitasking lifestyles. As Essafi, Belfakir, & Moubtassime (2024) in their study show, language learning applications, such as Duolingo, Babbel, Memrise, and HelloTalk, are among the most widely used tools by young learners. These applications incorporate elements of gamification, including points, badges, leaderboards, and progress tracking, to enhance motivation and engagement (Karasimos, 2022). Duolingo, in particular, is favoured by students for its user-friendly interface and short, interactive lessons that support spaced repetition and vocabulary acquisition (Febrianti et al., 2024). The recent rise of generative AI tools, especially ChatGPT, has added a new dimension to digital language learning. University students are increasingly using ChatGPT to understand grammar rules, generate sample texts, clarify complex vocabulary, and even practice simulated conversations (Du & Alm, 2024; Kavadella et al., 2024). These tools act as on-demand tutors, providing explanations and examples tailored to the learner's input. In a study by Hasanein and Sobaih (2023), over half of the students reported improved academic performance as a result of ChatGPT use, particularly in assignments involving reading comprehension and written production. Younger learners also frequently use multimedia platforms like YouTube, TikTok, and Instagram to access foreign language content, ranging from grammar tutorials to cultural insights (Nasution, 2022). Podcasts, music, and streaming services offer additional input-rich environments that support incidental learning and listening skills. Moreover, social media platforms and forums allow learners to join global communities where language is used authentically, contributing to increased exposure and communicative competence (Johnston et al., 2024).

Despite their digital fluency, young adults face challenges, such as over-reliance on technology, reduced critical thinking, and concerns about academic dishonesty (Ahadzadeh, Wu, & Sijia, 2024; Al-Zubaidi, Jaafari, & Touzani, 2024). Students often use AI tools without citing them, which raises ethical concerns around transparency and originality (Klimova & de Campos, 2024). Additionally, not all learners develop effective self-directed learning habits, leading to superficial engagement with digital tools (Uus, Mettis, & Väljataga, 2022).

To maximise the benefits of technology use among young adults, educators are encouraged to incorporate AI literacy into the curriculum, foster critical evaluation of digital content, and design assignments that promote deep learning and originality (Alrayes, Henari, & Ahmed, 2024). Institutions should also provide guidelines for ethical AI use and promote digital citizenship to ensure responsible engagement (Klimova, Pikhart & Kacetl, 2023).

Digital technologies in FLE and older adults

The engagement of older adults with digital technologies for foreign language learning has grown significantly in recent years, especially during and after the COVID-19 pandemic (Sixsmith et al., 2022). While older learners may encounter initial barriers, such as limited digital literacy, cognitive changes, or technophobia, research (Faverio, 2022; Klimova & Sanda, 2021) indicates that they are capable and willing to use technology provided that tools are accessible, beneficial, and socially meaningful.

Mobile apps, such as Duolingo, Babbel, Rosetta Stone, and Hello English have been tested among older populations with positive results. Duolingo, in particular, has emerged as a preferred app due to its simplicity, relevance to everyday communication, and intuitive interface (Meltzer et al., 2021; Puebla et al., 2021). As Klimova and Sanda (2021) in their study state, older users appreciate the short, goal-oriented lessons and immediate feedback that support independent learning and boost confidence. In addition to commercial apps, specialised applications such as Senioreng and SprachenTanz have been developed to cater specifically to the needs of older learners. These apps consider age-related factors such as cognitive processing speed, vision and hearing impairments, and motivation for social interaction. The SprachenTanz app, for example, was designed using a collaborative approach involving developers, educators, and older learners to ensure usability and relevance (Puebla et al., 2022).

Numerous studies (Gómez-Soria et al., 2023; Grossmann et al., 2023; Meltzer et al., 2021) have shown that FLE using digital tools contributes to cognitive stimulation among older adults. Language learning apps have been found to enhance executive functions, delay cognitive decline, and improve memory performance when compared with non-linguistic brain-training exercises. Furthermore, digital technologies enable older adults to remain socially connected. Language learning platforms with integrated chat features or peer collaboration options foster a sense of belonging and mitigate feelings of isolation (Puebla et al., 2021; Wang & Christiansen, 2019).

Unlike younger learners, older adults tend to prefer structured lessons with clear instructions, repetition, and explicit grammar explanations. They often appreciate blended learning formats that combine face-to-face instruction with digital tools. Challenges faced by this group include initial unfamiliarity with digital interfaces, anxiety about making mistakes, and limited exposure to English or other L2s earlier in life (Klimova & Sanda, 2021). However, when supported by user-friendly tutorials, peer mentoring, and appropriate design, older adults demonstrate resilience and adaptability in digital learning environments. Thus, for digital tools to be effective among older learners, they must align with the principles of age-friendly design. This includes readable fonts, auditory support, slow-paced navigation, and culturally relevant content. Moreover, instructional support, such as tutorials, help manuals, or in-person workshops, is crucial for building learners' confidence. Studies (Schiller, Dorner, & Szabó, 2023; van der Ploeg, Keijzer, & Lowie, 2023) emphasise the importance of personalised learning and social interaction as motivational drivers

Comparative analysis: Young vs older adults

While both young and older adults increasingly use digital technologies to support their foreign language learning (FLL), the ways in which they engage with these tools differ significantly. These differences stem from generational contrasts in digital literacy, cognitive preferences, social motivations, and pedagogical expectations. Young adults typically exhibit high frequency of digital technology use. They engage with a broad spectrum of applications, including mobile apps (e.g. Duolingo, Babbel), generative AI tools (e.g. ChatGPT), machine translation services (e.g. DeepL), and social media platforms (e.g. TikTok, Instagram, YouTube) for language exposure. Their usage patterns are characterised by multitasking, rapid content consumption, and gamified interaction (Karasimos, 2022; Singh, Tayarani-Najaran, & Yaqoob, 2023). Older adults, in contrast, are more selective in their technology use and generally favour applications that offer simplicity, clarity, and structure. While they also use Duolingo, Babbel, and Rosetta Stone, studies indicate that they are particularly receptive to apps developed with their specific cognitive and physical needs in mind, such as SprachenTanz or Senioreng (Puebla et al., 2022). They are less likely to experiment with unstructured tools, for example, ChatGPT unless guided by educators or digital literacy training (Klimova & Sanda, 2021).

Both age groups experience cognitive benefits from engaging in digital FLL. For young adults, the use of AI tools and interactive apps often improves vocabulary acquisition, reading comprehension, writing fluency, and task efficiency (Du & Alm, 2024; Kavadella et al., 2024). These tools serve as scaffolds that accelerate learning through real-time feedback and personalisation. For older adults, digital language learning supports not only linguistic development but also cognitive resilience. Engagement with mobile apps and structured digital courses has been shown to improve executive function, working memory, and processing speed (Grossmann et al., 2023; Meltzer et al., 2021;). The cognitive stimulation resulting from regular language practice may also help delay age-related cognitive decline (Klimova, 2020). However, while young adults often prioritise immediate academic gains, older learners value the long-term cognitive, emotional, and social outcomes of FLL. This difference underscores the need for age-sensitive learning objectives and tool design.

In addition, motivation for digital language learning varies across generations. Young adults are often motivated by academic performance, career advancement, international mobility, or peer recognition. Gamification elements, instant feedback, and the ability to track progress enhance their intrinsic and extrinsic motivation (Johnston et al., 2024; Duong, Vu & Ngo, 2023). In contrast, older adults are motivated by different factors: personal fulfilment, mental stimulation, a sense of purpose, and the opportunity for social interaction. Research shows that learners in this age group are more likely to persist when their emotional and social needs are addressed (Puebla et al., 2021; Schiller et al., 2023). For them, the community aspect of language learning, whether through peer learning, group chats, or social platforms integrated into apps, is essential.

Despite their fluency with technology, young adults face certain barriers, including the temptation to misuse AI tools (e.g. using ChatGPT to complete assignments without attribution), shallow engagement, and reduced critical thinking when overly dependent on digital assistance (Ahadzadeh, Wu, & Sijia, 2024). There are also growing concerns about data privacy, misinformation, and academic integrity (Magalhães Araujo & Cruz-Correia, 2024). For older adults, barriers are more often technical and affective in nature. These include low digital literacy, technophobia, accessibility issues (e.g. poor vision, limited dexterity), and limited exposure to foreign language education earlier in life (Zhang, 2023; Wang & Christiansen, 2019). However, these challenges can be mitigated with appropriate support structures such as training sessions, intuitive interfaces, and encouragement from facilitators.

Furthermore, young learners benefit from open-ended tasks, adaptive learning environments, and opportunities to explore content independently. However, the fast-paced nature of their learning style sometimes necessitates guidance to encourage deeper reflection and critical evaluation of AI-generated content (Alrayes, Henari, & Ahmed, 2024; Thelwall, 2024). Older learners, on the other hand, prefer structured, step-by-step learning with clear instructions, repetition, and teacher support. They value platforms that align with their pace and allow them to revisit content multiple times. Older adults also appreciate communicative approaches, especially when accompanied by explicit grammar explanations (van der Ploeg, Keijzer, & Lowie, 2023).

In both cases, successful pedagogical design requires tailoring content to learners' cognitive styles, goals, and preferences while ensuring digital tools are used ethically and effectively. Table 1 provides an overview of the key differences.

Table 1. Overview of the key differences in the use of digital technologies between young and older adults

Aspect	Young adults	Older adults
Technology use	Broad, experimental, multi-platform	Focused, cautious, user-friendly
Motivation	Academic performance, career, gamification	Cognitive stimulation, social connection, personal growth
Cognitive benefit	Efficiency, task automation, vocabulary gain	Memory improvement, delay of cognitive decline
Common tools	ChatGPT, Duolingo, social media, DeepL	Duolingo, SprachenTanz, Rosetta Stone
Challenges	Over-reliance, academic dishonesty, distraction	Technophobia, accessibility, digital literacy
Pedagogical needs	Adaptive, exploratory, AI literacy training	Structured, supportive, age-sensitive design

Benefits and limitations of the use of digital technologies in FLE

The integration of digital technologies in FLE has generated substantial benefits across age groups, but it also presents notable limitations that must be acknowledged and addressed.

Both younger and older learners experience significant cognitive gains through technology-supported FLL. For young adults, digital tools such as AI-powered writing assistants, grammar checkers, and translation engines enhance cognitive efficiency, supporting rapid comprehension and productive skill development (Hasanein & Sobaih, 2023). These tools allow students to engage in self-regulated learning, reflect on their linguistic choices, and explore complex ideas with scaffolding from generative AI (Du & Alm, 2024). Older adults, in turn, benefit cognitively through increased mental stimulation and executive function. Studies suggest that FLL via mobile apps contributes to improved memory, attention, and working memory, key aspects of healthy aging (Meltzer et al., 2021; Klimova & Sanda, 2021). Language learning also stimulates neuroplasticity, and when combined with digital tools, offers regular, accessible cognitive training (Grossmann et al., 2023).

Digital technologies enhance motivation through features, such as gamification, progress tracking, personalised feedback, and adaptive challenges. Younger learners, in particular, are drawn to the motivational aspects of apps like Duolingo and Babbel, which offer immediate rewards and performance indicators (Karasimos, 2022). Older adults, while less responsive to gamification, find motivation in the social and personal relevance of digital learning. Apps like SprachenTanz cater to these motivations by integrating social collaboration and culturally meaningful content (Puebla et al., 2022). This kind of learning promotes confidence and autonomy, especially when tailored to older learners' interests and experiences.

One of the major benefits of digital FLL tools is the flexibility they offer. Learners can access content anytime, anywhere, allowing for self-paced study and repeated exposure, essential for language acquisition. This flexibility benefits both students with busy academic schedules and older learners managing health, mobility, or lifestyle constraints (Wang & Christiansen, 2019; Klimova, 2020). Moreover, AI-driven tools like ChatGPT provide real-time explanations, summaries, and examples, acting as a virtual tutor for learners of all ages (Kavadella et al., 2024). These tools are especially valuable in informal learning contexts, supporting lifelong education outside institutional frameworks.

For older adults, digital technologies help combat social isolation by fostering interaction with peers and educators. Participating in online language courses, using chat features in apps, or attending virtual speaking groups fosters a sense of community (Puebla et al., 2021). As Sen, Prybutok, and Prybutok (2022) expand, such interactions not only support language practice but also promote emotional well-being. However, young adults also benefit from social learning, particularly when digital platforms are integrated with collaborative tasks, discussion forums, or peer-review systems (Ansari & Khan, 2020). Social media offers additional avenues for real-world language use and cultural immersion, enhancing communicative competence.

Nevertheless, there are also numerous challenges, which both young and older adults must face. Among young learners, one of the most cited concerns is over-reliance on AI tools like ChatGPT for completing assignments, generating ideas, or translating texts. This dependence may lead to surface-level learning, reduced problem-solving skills, and diminished originality (Ahadzadeh, Wu, & Sijia, 2024; Singh, Tayarani-Najaran, & Yaqoob, 2023). Furthermore, unchecked AI use can blur the lines between assistance and academic dishonesty, particularly when students fail to cite AI-generated input (Klimova & de Campos, 2024). Older learners, while increasingly engaged with digital learning tools, face more pronounced access barriers. These include low levels of digital literacy, technophobia, limited access to devices, and physical impairments such as vision or hearing difficulties (Zhang, 2023; Chu et al., 2022). Without proper support, such barriers can hinder learning, discourage participation, and reinforce educational inequalities. Even younger learners may face disparities in access to devices or high-speed internet, particularly in underserved regions or lower-income contexts (Afzal et al., 2023). As a result, the benefits of digital language learning are not equally distributed across all populations. While many apps and tools are designed for intuitive use, they often prioritise younger, tech-savvy users. Older adults may struggle with overly complex interfaces, small fonts, unclear instructions, or non-intuitive navigation (Klimova & Sanda, 2021). Moreover, many apps lack customisation for visual or auditory impairments, limiting accessibility.

There is also a lack of localisation and personalisation in some platforms, which may fail to reflect the linguistic, cultural, or cognitive preferences of older users. Generic content and fast-paced lessons can frustrate learners who prefer gradual, context-rich instruction. The widespread use of AI tools in FLL raises concerns about data privacy, bias, and transparency. Learners of all ages may be unaware of how their data is collected, stored, or used by AI systems (Feretzakis et al., 2024). This is particularly troubling for older adults, who may feel vulnerable in digital environments, and for institutions seeking to uphold academic integrity.

In addition, Klimova, Pikhart, and Kacetl (2023) claim that ethical concerns arise when learners use generative AI without understanding its limitations, such as hallucinated responses, lack of citation, or cultural insensitivity. Institutions and educators must address these risks by embedding digital ethics into curricula and fostering responsible technology use. Table 2 summarizes the main benefits and limitations of the use of digital technologies in FLE.

Table 2. Benefits and limitations of the use of digital technologies in FLE

Category	Benefits	Limitations
Cognitive	Improved memory, executive function, and language fluency	Superficial learning, cognitive overload
Motivational	Gamification, social relevance, personalised feedback	Overdependence on AI, reduced autonomy
Accessibility	Flexible, anytime learning, real-time support	Limited access for older adults or underserved populations
Social	Peer collaboration, reduced isolation, intercultural exchange	Lack of community features in many apps
Design and usability	User-friendly apps for younger learners	Inadequate age-friendly design for older learners
Ethical	Self-regulated learning, tutoring alternatives	Privacy concerns, academic dishonesty, AI bias

Pedagogical implications

The integration of digital technologies into FLE presents a valuable opportunity to modernise pedagogy and expand access to language learning across generations. However, these opportunities must be supported by age-sensitive, inclusive, and ethically grounded teaching practices. A one-size-fits-all approach to digital language learning is unlikely to meet the divergent needs of young and older adults. Educators must consider learners' age, background, digital literacy levels, and cognitive preferences when designing learning experiences.

For younger learners, instruction can benefit from:

- Adaptive learning platforms that personalise instruction and difficulty levels.
- Gamified tasks that maintain engagement and promote language retention.
- Project-based activities that involve real-world language use and problem-solving.
- Critical AI literacy modules that teach students how to evaluate, cite, and ethically use AI tools like ChatGPT (Thelwall, 2024; Alrayes, Henari, & Ahmed, 2024).

For older learners, instruction should include:

- Structured, step-by-step tasks with clear objectives and consistent design.
- Repetitive practice and explicit grammar instruction, which older learners often prefer (van der Ploeg, Keijzer, & Lowie, 2023).

- Age-friendly digital environments with accessible fonts, auditory support, and intuitive navigation (Klimova & Sanda, 2021).
- Face-to-face or video-based onboarding sessions to increase confidence in using digital tools.

These differentiated strategies ensure that each age group receives instruction that is not only technologically appropriate but also pedagogically effective. Digital literacy remains a prerequisite for the successful use of technology in FLE. While younger learners are often assumed to be digitally fluent, research (Bouzar et al., 2024; Essien et al., 2024) indicates that they may lack the critical skills needed to evaluate, apply, or reflect on the use of AI tools in learning. Similarly, older learners may struggle with basic operations or interface navigation.

To address these challenges, educators should:

- include digital skills training into the curriculum for all learners, covering tool selection, information evaluation, and digital ethics (Vuorikari, Pokropek, & Muñoz, 2025),
- provide video tutorials, manuals, and helplines to support technology adoption, especially for older learners (Klimova & Sanda, 2021),
- use peer mentoring or intergenerational learning models, where younger learners can help older adults navigate digital platforms, fostering mutual benefit and social inclusion (Juris et al., 2022),
- equip learners with the necessary digital skills not only support FLE outcomes but also promote broader educational equity (EU, 2020).

Effective pedagogy must also nurture learner motivation and autonomy, both of which are closely linked to successful language acquisition in digital contexts. For young adults, this means (Némethová, 2020):

- designing tasks that allow personal expression and creativity, reducing over-reliance on automated tools,
- encouraging goal-setting and self-assessment to build metacognitive awareness,
- incorporating collaborative digital projects to support peer interaction and communicative competence.

For older adults, pedagogical strategies should:

- emphasise the practical benefits of learning, such as travel or cultural engagement, to increase relevance (Ahmad et al., 2022).

- promote confidence and enjoyment, especially in learners returning to formal education after a long gap (Schiller, Dorner, & Szabó, 2023).
- integrate social learning components, such as discussion forums or group challenges, to reduce isolation and enhance motivation (Puebla et al., 2022).

Educators must also address the ethical dimensions of digital FLL. AI tools, if used uncritically, can promote plagiarism, misinformation, and inequality. To create responsible and inclusive digital learning environments, institutions and educators should:

- develop clear policies on the ethical use of AI tools and enforce citation requirements for AI-assisted work (George Pallivathukal et al., 2024),
- design AI-resistant assessments, such as oral exams, in-class discussions, or process-based writing assignments, to promote authentic learning (Singh, Tayarani-Najaran, & Yaqoob, 2023),
- raise awareness of data privacy, especially among older learners who may be more vulnerable to online threats (Feretzakis & Verykios, 2024),
- audit and adapt platforms to ensure that content, feedback, and interaction are free from algorithmic bias and inclusive of diverse linguistic and cultural backgrounds (Reiss, 2021).

The successful integration of digital technologies into language education requires institutional support and ongoing faculty training. Many instructors report feeling underprepared to use AI tools effectively or to guide students in doing so (Lee et al., 2024). Chardonnens (2025) suggests that institutions should therefore:

- offer professional development on emerging technologies, AI literacy, and inclusive pedagogy,
- foster cross-disciplinary collaboration among educators, technologists, and curriculum designers,
- create centres for digital innovation and ethics to guide best practices in technology-enhanced learning,
- invest in inclusive infrastructure, including age-friendly software, multilingual content, and technical support services.

Future perspectives

As digital technologies continue to evolve at a rapid pace, their role in FLE will only become more prominent and complex. The growing adoption of artificial intelligence (AI), virtual and augmented reality (VR/AR), and personalised learning systems signals a shift toward more dynamic, adaptive, and inclusive language learning environments. AI is already transforming language learning through tools, such as intelligent tutoring systems, generative language models, and adaptive learning platforms. Moving forward, AI's role in FLE is likely to expand in several areas:

- conversational AI and chatbots: tools, such as ChatGPT or language-specific chatbots can simulate immersive conversational experiences, providing learners with real-time speaking and listening practice (Adamopoulou & Moussiades, 2020; Klimova & Pikhart, 2022),
- AI-powered feedback: enhanced error correction and pronunciation analysis tools can provide immediate, personalised feedback beneficial to both beginner and advanced learners (Mohammed & Khalid, 2025),
- data-driven personalisation: AI can tailor content based on learners' pace, preferences, and performance, creating individualised learning paths that adapt over time (Ghafar et al., 2023).

However, as these tools become more sophisticated, ensuring their responsible and ethical use will be essential. Transparent algorithms, inclusive content, and protection of user data, especially for older learners, must remain priorities (Klimova, Pikhart, & Kacetl, 2023).

While many digital tools cater to tech-savvy users, future developments must prioritise universal design, making digital language education accessible to all users, regardless of age, ability, or background. Arora et al. (2024) then propose that key design features for inclusive platforms should include:

- scalable fonts and high-contrast visuals,
- audio-supported navigation and captioned content,
- multilingual interfaces and culturally adaptive material,
- adjustable learning speeds and simplified navigation structures.

Developers must work closely with educators, gerontologists, and accessibility experts to ensure that emerging platforms are not only technologically advanced but also genuinely inclusive (Klimova & Sanda, 2021).

Virtual reality (VR) and augmented reality (AR) technologies are becoming more viable for educational use and are expected to enhance language immersion in the coming years. Potential applications include (Zhao, Ren, & Cheah, 2023):

- virtual language labs: learners can enter simulated real-world environments (e.g. restaurants, airports, job interviews) to practice situational language use,
- cultural immersion: AR tools could bring cultural landmarks, traditions, or dialogues into learners' homes, making language learning more vivid and meaningful,
- gamified missions: learners can engage in role-playing games or quests that require them to solve problems in a foreign language context, increasing motivation and retention.

While younger learners may adapt quickly to these tools, older adults may require more structured onboarding and tailored design to feel comfortable using immersive environments.

As technology becomes inseparable from education, institutional and national policies must evolve to regulate the use of digital tools in FLE. Key policy areas include:

- AI use guidelines: clear frameworks are needed to guide the ethical integration of AI in language education, including standards for transparency, attribution, and academic honesty (Reiss, 2021; Wang et al., 2024),
- data protection: policies must ensure that learners' personal and learning data are securely stored, particularly given the sensitive nature of biometric and speech data used in some AI applications (Feretzakis & Verykios, 2024),
- funding for accessibility: public and private investment should prioritise the development of tools and resources that serve marginalised populations, including older learners, rural communities, and individuals with disabilities.

Ongoing research is needed to evaluate the effectiveness of emerging technologies across diverse learner populations. Future studies should:

- include older adults as key participants, ensuring their experiences inform tool development and pedagogy,
- assess long-term outcomes of digital language learning, including retention, fluency, and cognitive health,
- compare generational impacts of technologies, such as AI tutors, VR simulations, and mobile apps,
- investigate affective variables, such as confidence, motivation, and social belonging in tech-enhanced environments.

By expanding the scope and methodological rigour of FLE research, educators and developers can ensure that innovation aligns with evidence-based best practices.

The integration of digital technologies into foreign language education (FLE) has opened new possibilities for learners across the lifespan. As this chapter has shown, both young and older adults are engaging with digital tools to enhance their language learning experiences – albeit in different ways, for different reasons, and with different pedagogical needs. While young adults often gravitate toward mobile apps, AI tools, and multimedia platforms for their speed, flexibility, and interactivity, older learners increasingly turn to age-friendly applications and guided platforms that support cognitive health, social engagement, and personal growth.

The benefits of digital language learning are significant and well-documented. For young learners, these include improved efficiency, autonomy, and task performance. For older adults, foreign language learning supported by technology offers cognitive stimulation, a sense of purpose, and an avenue for social inclusion. Across both age groups, digital tools have democratised access to language learning, enabling self-paced, context-rich, and personalised educational experiences.

However, these benefits are accompanied by important limitations. Young adults face challenges such as over-reliance on AI, reduced critical thinking, and academic integrity concerns, while older learners must navigate digital barriers such as technophobia, accessibility issues, and cognitive load. These generational differences call for responsive pedagogical strategies that take into account learners' motivations, backgrounds, and preferred learning styles.

Pedagogically, this means moving beyond generic digital content toward inclusive, age-sensitive, and ethically grounded approaches. For younger learners, emphasis should be placed on AI literacy, ethical usage, and deeper engagement. For older learners, tailored content, scaffolded support, and user-friendly design are essential. Educators must also be supported with institutional training, policy frameworks, and ethical guidance to make the most of emerging technologies in the classroom.

Looking ahead, the future of digital FLE lies in fostering innovation that is both technologically advanced and socially inclusive. Advances in AI, virtual reality, and adaptive learning hold great promise, but only if developed in dialogue with diverse learners and grounded in research. Intergenerational models of learning, universal design, and the responsible integration of immersive technologies will shape the next chapter of language education.

Ultimately, the success of digital language learning across generations depends on collaboration among learners, educators, developers, and policymakers. By ensuring that digital tools are accessible, effective, and equitable, we can create lifelong learning ecosystems that empower individuals of all ages to communicate, connect, and thrive in an increasingly multilingual world.

CHAPTER 3

Cognitive gain in digital language learning

This chapter explores the potential of digital language learning in contributing to students' cognitive gains. It reviews existing research on the relationship between digital language learning and cognitive benefits, focusing on enhanced problem-solving skills, memory, and multitasking ability. The findings indicate that higher levels of digital competences correlate positively with language proficiency outcomes, suggesting that participants with greater digital skills achieve better language learning outcomes. Digital technologies offer interactive and engaging methods of learning, which can positively impact retention and understanding. However, the chapter also acknowledges the limitations of digital foreign language learning, such as the lack of face-to-face interaction and the need for high motivation and discipline. The research questions explored are: (1) Does digital language learning contribute to cognitive gains in foreign language education? and (2) What are the pedagogical implications for cognitive improvement in digital foreign language education? The results suggest that working with printed texts may be more effective for cognitive gains compared to electronic texts. Additionally, implementing more senses through digital language education appears to be beneficial for cognitive gains. The chapter concludes by discussing the implications of these findings and the need for further research in this area.

Digital technologies and cognitive abilities

Research conducted by Poláková & Klímová (2022) and Zhang (2021) demonstrates that learning a foreign language can significantly enhance cognitive abilities, leading to improvements in problem-solving skills, memory, and multitasking capabilities, regardless of age (Klimova & Pikhart, 2020). Studies have found that digital competences are positively correlated with language proficiency outcomes.

Participants who possess higher levels of digital competences tend to achieve better language learning results compared to those with lower levels (cf. Cao, Bhuvaneswari, Arumugam, & Aravind, 2023). Additionally, digital technologies provide interactive and engaging learning methods, which can enhance retention and understanding more effectively than traditional approaches (Park, 2022; Shafiee Rad, Roohani, & Rahimi Domakani, 2021; Yang, Yin, & Wang, 2018).

As previously mentioned, digital technology can positively impact cognitive skill development at any age. For instance, a study by Di Giacomo, Ranieri, and Lacasa (2017) involving 191 children aged 7 to 10 years revealed that exposure to digital gaming significantly improved their learning capabilities. This improvement was not only evident in their educational success but also in their cognitive functionality, particularly in verbal and visuoperceptual performance. Similar findings were observed among older individuals, where computer-based foreign language training programs contributed to cognitive benefits, especially in enhancing cognitive functions such as working memory (cf. Klimova, 2021).

Moreover, the integration of digital technologies into foreign language teaching and learning has become a popular method of language acquisition (Bećirović, Brdarević-Čeljo, & Delić, 2021). These technologies offer easy and rapid access to diverse linguistic resources, teaching tools, and community interactions. They enable learners to progress at their own pace, from any location and at any time, making learning more personalised (Haleem, Javaid, Qadri, & Suman, 2022) and fostering self-directed learning (Bancha & Tongtep, 2021). Consequently, this leads to more effective learning outcomes (Lai et al., 2022).

Overall, the implementation of digital technologies in foreign language education provides numerous benefits, including access to a wide range of resources, interactive teaching tools, community interactions, personalised and self-directed learning, and improved learning effectiveness (Ng et al., 2023). These advantages have made digital technologies a favoured method for language acquisition in contemporary educational settings.

However, digital foreign language learning also presents certain limitations. The absence of face-to-face interaction can hinder the consolidation of some linguistic phenomena that are typically reinforced in traditional classroom settings (Gherheş, Stoian, Fărcaşiu, & Stanici, 2021). Additionally, the self-directed nature of digital learning demands a high level of motivation and discipline, which can be challenging for some learners (Zamborová, Stefanutti, & Klimová, 2021). Research also suggests that technology may not always contribute to cognitive gains. For example, a Finnish study (Saarinen et al., 2021) investigating the use of information and communications technology (ICT) in secondary schools among 5,037 students found that frequent ICT use was associated with weaker performance in all cognitive learning outcomes.

Recognising these limitations can help educators and learners make informed decisions regarding the appropriate use of digital technologies in foreign language education. A balanced approach that combines digital resources with face-to-face interactions and effective pedagogical strategies can help mitigate these limitations and provide a comprehensive language learning experience.

Cognitive gain while using digital technologies

The research into the topic of cognitive gain when using digital media for foreign language learning is scarce but still there are a few studies that demonstrate that the topic is relevant. The results of recent studies highlight two significant outcomes. Firstly, working with printed texts appears to be more effective for cognitive gains compared to electronic texts. This finding is supported by research conducted by Chiu and Liu (2013), Mangen, Anda, Oxborough, and Brřnnick (2015), and Pikhart, Klimova, and Ruschel (2023). Chiu and Liu (2013) examined the impact of using printed dictionaries, pocket electronic dictionaries, and online type-in dictionaries on English vocabulary retention among 33 seventh graders in Taiwan. Their findings indicated that while electronic dictionaries temporarily attract students' attention, printed dictionaries help retain target words more effectively. Similarly, Mangen et al. (2015) explored the impact of writing modality on word recall and recognition among 36 females in Norway, finding that handwriting led to significantly better free recall of words compared to keyboard writing conditions. Pikhart et al. (2023) evaluated vocabulary retention in L2 using print text versus digital media among 122 university students in the Czech Republic and Brazil, concluding that students using print text performed better in vocabulary memory post-tests. These studies suggest that printed materials help learners retain information more effectively, possibly due to the tactile and visual engagement they provide.

Secondly, incorporating multiple senses through digital foreign language education seems to be beneficial for cognitive gains. Studies by Bancha and Tongtep (2021), Park (2022), Roussel and Galan (2018), Shafiee Rad, Roohani, and Rahimi Domakani (2021), and Yang, Yin, and Wang (2018) indicate that engaging multiple senses can enhance the learning experience and improve retention and understanding. For example, Park (2022) studied the impact of a technology-enhanced real-world environment on foreign vocabulary acquisition among 48 adult participants of various nationalities in the UK. The study found that engaging all senses in a technology-enhanced environment is more effective for vocabulary learning than using only a few senses. Bancha and Tongtep (2021) explored whether vocabulary lessons combined with LMS exercises and MultiEx games could enhance short-term vocabulary memorisation and long-term retention among 72 first-year Thai students. The results showed that the MultiEx game group had higher mean scores in both immediate and delayed post-tests, although both groups improved their language proficiency. Roussel and Galan (2018) examined the effect of clicker use to support learning in a dual-focused second language German course among 36 Law School students in France. The clicker group outperformed the non-clicker group in a post-test concerning legal terminology, illustrating that clicker use enhances cognitive load and learning. Shafiee Rad et al. (2021) assessed the effectiveness of a technology-enhanced flipped classroom on English language learners' expository writing skills among 60 female students in Iran. The experimental groups, particularly the role-reversal group, showed more significant writing gains compared to the control group. Yang et al. (2018) explored the application of the flipped learning approach in teaching Chinese as a foreign language among two first-year Chinese classes in the USA. The flipped class outperformed the traditional class in speaking skills. These studies collectively indicate that engaging multiple senses through digital technologies can enhance cognitive gains in foreign language learning.

L2 acquisition and cognitive gain

In Thailand, Bancha and Tongtep (2021) explored whether vocabulary lessons combined with LMS exercises and MultiEx games could enhance short-term vocabulary memorisation and long-term retention among 72 first-year Thai students. The study involved two groups: one group received face-to-face lessons combined with LMS exercises, while the other group received face-to-face lessons combined with MultiEx games. The participants, who had a low level of English proficiency, were tested using the Test of English for International Communication (TOEIC) over a period of 10 weeks. The results showed that the MultiEx game group had higher mean scores in both immediate and delayed post-tests, although both groups improved their language proficiency. This suggests that interactive and engaging methods, such as digital games, can enhance vocabulary retention and overall language proficiency.

Chiu and Liu (2013) examined the impact of using printed dictionaries, pocket electronic dictionaries, and online type-in dictionaries on English vocabulary retention among 33 seventh graders in Taiwan. The participants were asked to use all three types of dictionaries to complete reading tasks consisting of three articles, each 200 words long, adapted from a widely used English learning magazine published in Taiwan. The study employed pre-tests, immediate post-tests, delayed post-tests of vocabulary, questionnaires, and interviews to evaluate the effectiveness of each dictionary type. The findings indicated that while electronic dictionaries temporarily attract students' attention, printed dictionaries help retain target words more effectively. This suggests that traditional printed materials may be more effective for long-term vocabulary retention.

Liao, Kruger, and Doherty (2020) investigated the impact of bilingual subtitles on cognitive load and comprehension in L2 among 20 Chinese native postgraduate students in Australia. The participants, who used English as their second language, were divided into four groups: one group watched videos with English narration and Chinese subtitles, another group watched videos with English narration and English subtitles, a third group watched videos with both Chinese and English subtitles, and the fourth group watched videos without subtitles. The study employed biographical questionnaires, cognitive load questionnaires, eye tracking, and statistical processing to evaluate the impact of subtitles on cognitive load and comprehension. The findings indicated that bilingual subtitles provide linguistic support, making videos easier to comprehend without causing cognitive overload. This suggests that subtitles can enhance comprehension and facilitate the learning process without impeding cognitive function.

Mangen, Anda, Oxborough, and Brřnnick (2015) explored the impact of writing modality on word recall and recognition among 36 females aged 19–54 years in Norway. The participants, who were college students or staff at a middle-sized Norwegian university, were required to use handwriting, a physical laptop keyboard, and an iPad virtual touch keyboard to write down different word lists. The study employed a word list paradigm and statistical processing to evaluate the effectiveness of each writing modality. The results showed that handwriting led to significantly better free recall of words compared to both keyboard writing conditions. This suggests that traditional handwriting may be more effective for long-term word recall and recognition.

Park (2022) studied the impact of a technology-enhanced real-world environment on foreign vocabulary acquisition among 48 adult participants of various nationalities living in Newcastle, UK. The participants, aged between 19 and 49 years, had two cooking sessions: one in a kitchen using real objects and the other in a classroom looking at photos. All participants were learning basic Korean. The study employed pre-tests, immediate post-tests, delayed post-tests, and statistical processing to evaluate the effectiveness of each learning environment. The findings indicated that engaging all senses in a technology-enhanced environment is more effective for vocabulary learning than using only a few senses. This suggests that immersive and interactive environments can enhance vocabulary acquisition and overall language proficiency.

Pikhart, Klimova, and Ruschel (2023) evaluated vocabulary retention in L2 using print text versus digital media among 122 university students in the Czech Republic and Brazil. The participants, who had a level of English proficiency ranging from B2 to C1 according to the Common European Reference Framework for languages, were divided into two groups to learn sixty new phrasal verbs over a period of 4 weeks. One group used a standard print text, while the other group used the same text displayed and annotated on their digital devices. The study employed vocabulary memory post-tests and statistical processing to evaluate the effectiveness of each learning method. The findings indicated that students using print text performed better in both tests. This suggests that traditional printed materials may be more effective for long-term vocabulary retention.

Roussel and Galan (2018) examined the effect of clicker use to support learning in a dual-focused second language German course among 36 Law School students in France. The participants, who had a level of German proficiency ranging from B1 to C1, answered questions with or without clicker use during the 10-week semester. Five sessions were conducted with clickers and five sessions without. The study employed pre-tests and post-test questionnaires, and statistical processing to evaluate the effectiveness of clicker use. The findings indicated that the clicker group outperformed the non-clicker group in a post-test concerning legal terminology. This suggests that clicker use can enhance cognitive load and learning, particularly in dual-focused language courses.

Shafiee Rad, Roohani, and Rahimi Domakani (2021) assessed the effectiveness of a technology-enhanced flipped classroom on English language learners' expository writing skills among 60 female students in Iran. The participants, who had an advanced level of English proficiency, were divided into three groups: a control group, a discussion-oriented flipped group, and a role-reversal flipped group. The study employed English placement tests, pre-tests, post-tests, questionnaires, semi-structured interviews, and statistical processing to evaluate the effectiveness of each learning method. The findings indicated that the experimental groups were more effective than the control group in writing gains, with the role-reversal group outperforming the discussion-oriented group. This suggests that technology-enhanced flipped classrooms can enhance expository writing skills and overall language proficiency.

Yang, Yin, and Wang (2018) explored the application of the flipped learning approach in teaching Chinese as a foreign language among two first-year Chinese classes in the USA. One class followed a traditional face-to-face learning approach with nine students, while the other class used a flipped (online) learning approach with eight students. The study spanned one semester and employed the Oxford Language Aptitude Test, Chinese placement test, final oral and written tests, and questionnaires to evaluate the effectiveness of each learning method. The findings indicated that students in the flipped class outperformed those in the traditional class in speaking skills. This suggests that the flipped learning approach, which allows students to engage with instructional content at their own pace outside of class and use class time for interactive activities, can enhance speaking skills and overall language proficiency.

These studies collectively provide valuable insights into the cognitive benefits of digital foreign language education and highlight the importance of incorporating multiple senses and traditional methods to enhance learning outcomes. By understanding the strengths and limitations of different learning modalities, educators can design more effective language learning programmes that cater to the diverse needs of learners. The integration of digital technologies, when combined with traditional methods, can create a balanced and comprehensive language learning experience that maximises cognitive gains and language proficiency.

Summary of the current research findings

The findings from the current research indicate that the cognitive benefits of digital foreign language learning are varied. Therefore, the answer to whether digital language learning contributes to cognitive gains in foreign language education is not definitive. The effectiveness of digital foreign language learning depends on several factors, including the learning method, students' needs, motivation, and the digital tools used. For instance, traditional pen and paper methods for retaining new vocabulary appear to be more effective than using language applications. Mangen, Anda, Oxborough, and Brřnnick (2015) highlight that writing with a pen involves different sensorimotor and kinesthetic processes compared to typing on a keyboard. Similarly, Umejima, Ibaraki, Yamazaki, and Sakai (2021) argue that handwriting facilitates the acquisition of rich encoding and spatial information. Pikhart, Klimova, and Ruschel (2023) also emphasise the importance of making notes, highlighting, or writing translations in one's native language for long-term retention. This is supported by Chiu and Liu (2013), who found that the fast retrieval speed of electronic dictionaries might hinder word retention.

In summary, the relationship between digital foreign language learning and cognitive gains is complex and influenced by various factors. The effectiveness of digital language learning in enhancing cognition depends on the learning approach, individual needs, motivation, and the specific digital tools used.

Activities such as taking notes, highlighting, or writing translations can significantly improve long-term vocabulary retention (Pikhart, Klimova, & Ruschel, 2023). Additionally, printed dictionaries have shown greater efficacy than electronic ones, as the quick retrieval speed of electronic resources may impede word retention (Chiu & Liu, 2013).

On the other hand, the techniques and strategies employed for learning a foreign language play a crucial role. For example, digital games have been found to be beneficial, as shown by Bancha and Tongtep (2021). This aligns with Vnucko and Klimova (2023), who state that digital games create a positive emotional environment that can enhance vocabulary retention. Huang, Willson, and Eslami (2012) also report that games stimulate learning and help students maintain attention during vocabulary lessons. Park (2022) suggests that engaging multiple senses in language learning improves vocabulary retention. The flipped classroom approach, which has gained popularity, especially after the COVID-19 pandemic, allows teachers to focus on essential linguistic phenomena during class time, provided they offer adequate online support (Li & Li, 2022). The review findings indicate that the flipped classroom approach can improve both writing (Shafiee Rad, Roohani, & Rahimi Domakani, 2021) and speaking skills (Yang, Yin, & Wang, 2018).

The key takeaway is that the effectiveness of digital foreign language learning depends on the techniques and strategies used. Approaches such as digital games and the flipped classroom have shown potential benefits for cognitive improvement in language learning. Digital games create a positive emotional environment and enhance attention and retention of new words. Engaging multiple senses and providing online support can improve vocabulary retention. The flipped classroom approach, when adequately supported, has demonstrated cognitive improvements in both writing and speaking skills.

Pedagogical implications

There are several pedagogical implications for cognitive improvement in digital foreign language education, and the results of current research suggest the following:

- Implementing techniques or strategies that best suit students' language needs in a digital environment, whether it be pen and paper or a flipped classroom.
- Exposing students to multiple techniques that engage most of their senses, positively impacting cognitive gains.

- Providing students with feedback to keep them motivated in their language studies.
- Using appropriate techniques or strategies in a digital foreign language setting, such as pen and paper activities or a flipped classroom approach, tailored to meet individual language needs, helps ground students in a real setting.
- Exposing students to multiple techniques rather than relying on a single approach ensures engagement of various senses, maximising cognitive benefits.
- Providing feedback is crucial for maintaining motivation and encouraging language learning endeavours.

The limitations of this summary reflect a relatively small number of research studies on the topic. However, the findings of the available research are representative, including different regions and various digital tools used in foreign language learning to achieve cognitive gains. In summary, although empirical research is limited, it provides a preliminary basis for future studies. This chapter can serve as a catalyst for further research, given the widespread use of digital tools in learning, making it essential to explore their potential impact on cognitive development.

Conclusion

In conclusion, the findings of this chapter underscore the variability in cognitive gains associated with digital foreign language learning. The question of whether digital language learning contributes to cognitive improvement in foreign language education remains unresolved due to the advantages and disadvantages linked to various factors, such as learning methods, student needs, motivation, and the digital tools employed. While traditional pen and paper methods seem to be more effective for word retention compared to language applications, there is substantial evidence supporting the positive impact of digital games on vocabulary acquisition. Additionally, the flipped classroom approach shows potential in enhancing cognitive abilities in both writing and speaking skills.

Based on the results presented in this chapter, several pedagogical implications arise for fostering cognitive improvement in digital foreign language education. Firstly, it is essential to implement techniques and strategies that best meet students' language needs in a digital learning environment, whether through pen and paper activities or a flipped classroom approach. Secondly, exposing students to a variety of techniques that engage multiple senses can positively influence cognitive gains. Lastly, providing students with feedback is crucial to maintain their motivation and encourage ongoing progress in their foreign language studies.

Although this chapter has identified certain limitations, such as the limited availability of research studies in this area, the findings still provide a preliminary foundation for future investigations. As digital tools continue to play a significant role in learning, further research is necessary to explore their potential impact on cognitive development. Overall, this chapter serves as a starting point for future inquiries and highlights the need for continued exploration of digital foreign language education and its implications for cognitive enhancement.

Digital games: Theory and practice, trends, challenges and future directions

Introduction

Language instruction is revolutionised by technological innovation, which improves learning efficacy and accessibility (Jiang et al., 2022). Even if students are both subjectively satisfied and dissatisfied with the usage of digital media in their learning context, the recent unprecedented advancements in technology have expanded opportunities for language practice and socialisation (Pikhart et al., 2022). If students don't find class activities interesting or challenging enough, they are less likely to participate in them, especially in online classes (Al-Obaydi et al., 2023). Student motivation and engagement have been demonstrated to rise with the use of technology, including interactive tools and mobile applications (Hossain et al., 2024; Ryan & Deci, 2020). For instance, an experimental study that combined mobile applications with language instruction showed that, in comparison to the control group, students in the experimental group performed better and gave favourable comments (Mengorio & Dumlao, 2019).

Since the development of AI-powered tools and adaptive learning systems, teachers can now modify their lessons to fit the unique requirements of each student, taking into consideration differences in cognitive capacities and learning styles (Pikhart et al., 2024a). Applications of Howard Gardner's Theory of Multiple Intelligences have demonstrated that technology, when combined with individualised teaching strategies, improves language outcomes, especially in speaking and writing (Hu & Yuan, 2025).

Additionally, real-time cooperation made possible by technology helps students build their interpersonal skills and use language in meaningful ways. In order to promote genuine connection, online platforms and video conferencing tools are essential (Derakhshan, 2021). For instance, mobile-assisted language learning (MALL) gives students flexibility and autonomy by enabling them to access instructional materials at any time and from any location (Klimova & Al-Obaydi, 2023). Particularly in areas with restricted access to conventional resources, experimental studies demonstrate how well mobile learning can enhance language acquisition (Sophonhiranrak, 2021).

These developments highlight how crucial it is to use technology into language instruction in order to establish inclusive, stimulating, and productive learning environments. Visual aids improve understanding and memory even more (Al-Obaydi & Pikhart, 2022; Derakhshan, Eslami & Shakki, 2023). Incidental language exposure, which is any contact that reinforces previously learned material without a formal educational goal, can also be supported by technological activities. Leisure time language engagement opportunities combine learning and enjoyment, encouraging consistent practice and motivation (Liu et al., 2021; Soyoof et al., 2023).

A potent instructional tool that creatively combines learning and engagement is the digital game (Pikhart et al., 2024b). They aid in the development of dynamic settings where students can investigate ideas, hone abilities, and work through challenges. Through encouraging teamwork and critical thinking, games facilitate active learning (Soyoof et al., 2023). Students can experience real-world situations, like running a business or investigating ecosystems, for example, through simulation games (Tawafak et al., 2023). Furthermore, educational games enhance motivation and retention by making learning fun (Pikhart et al., 2024b). With their visual, aural, and kinesthetic components, they accommodate a variety of learning preferences. Additionally, pupils can receive tailored feedback from digital games, which can help them pinpoint their areas of weakness (Klimova & Kacetl, 2017). Their versatility has completely changed the way that education is taught, from teaching programming through coding challenges to enhancing language skills through word games (Tawafak et al., 2018).

Digital games have been shown to be effective in a variety of educational environments by experimental studies. When compared to conventional approaches, digital educational games dramatically improve STEM learning results, according to a meta-analytic evaluation by Gui et al. (2023). Additionally, game design components increase the instructional impact. Research on how kids utilise educational digital games emphasises how they help kids develop their ability to make decisions and solve problems (Çiftçi, 2018). These games are excellent resources for interactive engagement and practice-based learning. Khattib's quasi-experimental study highlighted the benefits of digital gamification in science teaching (2024). Students who used programs like CoSpaces Edu reported better levels of motivation, immersion, and engagement than those who received traditional in-person training.

Drawing on the discussion above, the current chapter attempts to demonstrate how digital games are transforming language instruction. Theoretical underpinnings, real-world applications, difficulties, and emerging trends will be dealt with extensively. The main questions that need a reply in this chapter are:

1. Which theoretical underpinnings influence the incorporation of digital games into language instruction, and what are the emerging research trends in this area of study?
2. What advantages, challenges, and practical applications are associated with the use of digital games in language teaching, and how may these issues be addressed in future directions?

Theoretical foundations

In relation to language teaching, a number of important learning theories that place an emphasis on interaction, motivation, and contextualised practice encourage the use of digital games in language instruction. The benefit of dynamic, learner-centred settings where students create meaning via investigation and problem-solving conditions that game-based learning naturally promotes is highlighted by constructivist theory (Plass et al., 2015). Digital games can improve intrinsic motivation by fostering autonomy, competence, and relatedness, according to Self-Determination Theory (SDT) (Pikhart et al., 2024b). This is particularly true when students feel emotionally invested and in charge of their own development. According to the Affective Filter Hypothesis, well-designed educational games can greatly enhance language acquisition by reducing fear and boosting enjoyment, two common results (Bailey & Fahad, 2021). Sociocultural theory also highlights the need of scaffolding and meaningful interaction, both of which games frequently offer through group projects and immediate feedback. Together, these theoretical stances promote the educational potential of digital games to give language learners rich, emotionally engaging, and linguistically stimulating environments.

The usefulness of using digital games in the classroom is supported by a number of important learning theories. Constructivism is one of these theories. Through experiences and introspection, students actively develop their own knowledge and understanding during the learning process. This theory holds that games frequently offer engaging, problem-solving settings that let students experiment, make decisions, and grow from the results of their choices. Because they promote critical thinking, teamwork, and the practical application of information, these activities are consistent with constructivist concepts (Plass et al., 2015). Another theoretical underpinning is Game-Based Learning (GBL), which refers to the use of real games as instructional aids in order to accomplish particular learning objectives (Adipat et al., 2021). Creating or using games with specific educational goals is emphasised by GBL. These games encourage the development of skills (such as problem-solving and cooperation) and comprehension of the material in an interesting and organic way (Plass et al., 2015). Another theoretical foundation for gamification is the idea that by incorporating game-like aspects (such as leaderboards, badges, and points) into non-gaming environments, engagement can be increased. By using incentives and competition, gamification encourages students and makes learning activities more interesting (Kapp, 2012). To maintain students' interest and motivation, game-based learning, on the other hand, frequently includes components like challenges, incentives, and feedback. This is a common application of self-determination theory, which stresses internal motivation (Pikhart et al., 2024b). In terms of cognitive development, games are made to improve memory retention, critical thinking, and problem-solving abilities (Mayer, 2019). They give students the chance to use what they've learned in simulated real-world situations (Granic et al., 2014). Online learning platforms ensure accessibility and scalability by delivering game-based learning using digital technologies (Tawafak et al., 2025).

With their alignment with theories such as Communicative Language Teaching (CLT) (Zhu, 2012), and Krashen's Input Hypothesis, digital games can be effective instruments for language acquisition (Bailey & Fahad, 2021). Krashen highlights the significance of understandable input, which is language that is only a little bit above the learner's present proficiency level ('i+1'). This is commonly accomplished through interactive conversations, visual assistance, and contextual clues in online education generally (Al-Obaydi & Pikhart, 2022), and digital games specifically (Xu et al., 2020). For instance, games with a narrative focus that draw players into stories and introduce them to new vocabulary and grammar in context, as well as multiplayer games that promote player interaction, expose learners to a variety of linguistic inputs, and promote comprehension in real time (Reinhardt & Thorne, 2020). Digital games can also lower the 'affective filter' (a notion from Krashen's theory) because they provide a fun, stress-free atmosphere for language acquisition. This increases students' openness to learning new language abilities (Xu et al., 2020). CLT, however, emphasises genuine engagement and communication. Role-playing games, which frequently require players to converse, negotiate, or solve problems using the target language, are examples of digital games that mimic real-life situations (Reinhardt, 2019). Promoting cooperation that playing multiplayer games helps students practice English in real-world situations while encouraging cooperation and communication and giving comments where instant feedback on language use is provided by many games, which strengthens learning and promotes self-correction as well (He, 2022).

In conclusion, digital games are useful resources for language learning since they are consistent with important theories like CLT and Krashen's Input

Hypothesis. By lowering affective filters, simulating real-world communication situations, and providing intelligible input, they promote cooperation and real-time interaction. A dynamic and captivating medium for language acquisition, games are enhanced by the incorporation of feedback mechanisms.

Trends in research: What is missing?

Research on digital games has expanded dramatically, especially in the educational contexts, and has become a lively and varied field of study. Researchers have investigated the ways in which digital games can be used as powerful instruments to increase motivation, engage students, and offer chances for immersive educational experiences (Adipat et al., 2021). The application of gamification concepts, like progression mechanisms and reward systems, has been shown to improve students' perseverance and attentiveness. Digital games can also help students develop critical thinking, cooperation, problem-solving, and teamwork skills that are crucial for learners in the twenty-first century, according to studies (Gros, 2007; Liu & Shadiev, 2025).

The primary focus of contemporary trends is motivation and engagement. Digital games improve intrinsic motivation and student engagement, according to numerous research (Alahmari et al., 2023; Krystalli & Arvanitis, 2024; Li et al., 2024; Pikhart et al., 2024b; Soyoof et al., 2023). Gamification principles, for instance, are extensively researched due to their capacity to maintain interest and enhance learning results (Alahmari et al., 2023). There is also a movement toward empirical studies on learning outcomes. Digital games' ability to enhance particular abilities, including problem-solving, critical thinking, or language learning, is frequently the subject of research (Ratnasari et al., 2023). The other trend is technological integration, which encompasses research that investigates the integration of technological innovations like virtual reality (VR) and augmented reality (AR) into game-based learning settings and the amount of time spent on skills development (Al-Obaydi et al., 2025; Gundersen & Lampropoulos, 2025; Liu & Shadiev, 2025).

There are still gaps in spite of these advancements. The long-term effects of digital games on learning outcomes and retention, for instance, have not been thoroughly studied (Al-Obaydi, Pikhart & Shakki, 2023; Lampropoulos & Sidiropoulos, 2024; Osman & Abdul Rabu, 2020). The efficiency of games for students from different socio-economic or cultural backgrounds is questioned because much research lacks demographic diversity (Gros, 2007). Furthermore, research on accessibility and scalability for underfunded educational institutions is still lacking, as is the integration of interdisciplinary approaches that combine ideas from psychology, technology, and education (Alahmari et al., 2023). Another gap is the lack of interdisciplinary studies integrating technology, psychology, and education; digital games are currently examined separately (Ratnasari et al., 2023). A more thorough examination is also needed in the ethical issues of addiction and data privacy (Kneer et al., 2014; Silva et al., 2023). Although research on digital games has advanced significantly overall, filling in these gaps could allow them to reach their full potential in revolutionising education for a wide range of international and diverse student populations. Table 3 summarises the current trends of research on the use of digital games in language instruction and points out areas that require more investigation:

Table 3. Summary of the current trends of research on the use of digital games and what is missing

Current trends	What is missing
Pay attention to gamification to improve language learning motivation and engagement.	Few studies have examined the long-term effects on language memory and proficiency.
Research on the use of serious games to improve communication skills.	Absence of studies on localising games for various learners and cultural sensitivity.
Using game-based applications to support mobile-assisted language learning (MALL).	Inadequate evaluation of resources or accessibility for students with impairments.
Commercial off-the-shelf (COTS) games used to increase vocabulary.	Few studies have examined the efficacy of tailored educational games against COTS games.
Investigations into feedback systems in game-based learning settings.	Insufficient emphasis on preparing teachers to include digital games into the curriculum.

Advantages of digital games in language teaching

By encouraging participation, offering contextualised feedback, and mimicking real-world communication situations, digital games improve language instruction. Through their multiplayer capabilities, they promote teamwork and give language learners interactive opportunity to develop their language skills (Tawafak et al., 2025). Additionally, games give players instant feedback, which helps them improve their skills while lowering stress and increasing motivation (Alamer, 2016; Pikhart et al., 2024b). Digital games can also help students better understand the target language by exposing them to its cultural nuances (Al-Obaydi, Pikhart & Shakki, 2023). Studies like He's Review in Language Learning & Technology (2022) and Reinhardt and Thorne's work (2020) support these advantages.

It has been demonstrated that digital games increase motivation and participation in a variety of settings, most notably in education and personal growth (Alamer, 2016). Due to the fact that online games are by their nature engaging and interactive, players are drawn in and remain interested (Soyoof et al., 2021). Traditional approaches frequently lack the sense of engagement that is created by the use of captivating storylines, challenges, and incentives. For instance, by adding aspects of enjoyment and competition, educational games can increase the attraction of learning (He, 2022). Intrinsic motivation can be increased by games' frequent instant feedback and rewards, such levels, badges, or points (Fulya Eyupoglu & Nietfeld, 2019). The players' sense of accomplishment and advancement motivates them to keep playing. Additionally, people may choose their own pace and goals thanks to the autonomy and control that games provide, which further boosts motivation (Al-Obaydi, Pikart & Klimova, 2023).

Experimental research has shown that digital games present special chances for genuine communication and cultural awareness. Real-time player interaction is facilitated by digital games, particularly those that are online and multiplayer (Al-Obaydi et al., 2025). As players cooperate, plan, and interact, this promotes genuine communication. For instance, research has demonstrated that by offering interesting and dynamic environments, digital games can improve the communication readiness of English as a Foreign Language (EFL) learners (Bagherpour et al., 2022). On the other hand, games frequently include a variety of cultural components, including customs, dialects, and historical accounts (Cerezo-Pizarro et al., 2023). This gives players an immersive opportunity to experience and learn about various civilisations. The cultural impact of video games has been thoroughly examined in research, with a focus on how these games promote global understanding and cultural transmission (Cerezo-Pizarro et al., 2023). Additionally, digital games are increasingly recognised as platforms for cultural and educational transmission. They give gamers a chance to investigate cultural variety and have deep cross-cultural conversations (Cui, 2016).

It has been demonstrated that playing digital games helps players develop their critical thinking and problem-solving abilities by providing them with dynamic, captivating environments that test their ability to assess circumstances, make choices, and modify their approach (Gundersen & Lampropoulos, 2025). Digital and serious games have been shown to dramatically improve students' computational thinking and problem-solving abilities in K–12 settings (Gundersen & Lampropoulos, 2025). These games encourage self-regulated learning, enhance engagement, and offer interactive learning experiences in language learning (Soyoof et al., 2021). According to Dehghanzadeh (2021), specific game elements, like genre and mechanics, have been shown to improve children's and adolescents' critical thinking and problem-solving abilities in studies looking into the connection between video game design and critical thinking.

By offering individualised learning experiences, digital games have shown to be flexible enough to accommodate different learners' skill levels. Digital games were found to improve learning outcomes and self-efficacy by adjusting to the emotional states and skill levels of learners (Chen & Tu, 2021). Digital games like Kahoot have been shown to dramatically increase students' interest and learning performance in English language classrooms (Hossain & Al Younus, 2024). The study by Wichadee & Pattanapichet (2018) highlighted how digital games may be tailored to various skill levels, increasing student engagement. A framework for instructional games that adjust to the skill levels of learners was presented in another study. It emphasised how gaming components promote social and cognitive abilities, guaranteeing chances for lifelong learning (Adipat et al., 2021).

In conclusion, by fostering dynamic and captivating learning settings, digital games provide a number of benefits for language instruction, see Table 4. They guarantee cognitive development, individualised learning experiences by boosting motivation, offering immediate feedback, enhanced memory, and adjusting to students' skill levels. These activities also increase teamwork, sharpen problem-solving abilities, and enhance the fun and efficiency of language learning.

Table 4. Overview of the advantages of digital games in a variety of fields

Category	Benefits	Description
Cognitive Development	Improved Critical Thinking and Problem-Solving Skills	Playing games helps players think strategically, assess situations, and adjust to changing obstacles.
Hand-Eye Coordination	Enhanced Motor Abilities	Playing simulation and action games helps users learn to coordinate their motor reactions with visual input.
Memory and Attention	Improved Concentration and Memory	Players frequently have to concentrate on goals and retain facts, which strengthens cognitive abilities.
Social Interaction	Cooperation as well as Teamwork	Through cooperation, multiplayer and internet games promote social skills and communication.
Educational Outcomes	Engaging Education	Through captivating content, educational games enhance language, numeracy, and reading abilities.
Emotional Well-Being	Mood Enhancement and Stress Reduction	Playing video games lowers stress levels by promoting relaxation and a sense of achievement.

Types of digital games used in language teaching

There are many different types of digital games used in language instruction, each one created to meet the demands of the student and particular educational objectives, see Table 5. These consist of immersive role-playing games that foster communication skills, serious vocabulary and grammar-focused games, and interactive simulations for practice in real-world situations. Along with improving language skills, puzzle-based games frequently improve critical thinking, and multiplayer games encourage cooperation and cross-cultural interaction among students. Language instruction can be enhanced in a variety of ways with these varied game kinds (Alyaz & Genc, 2016; Otero De Juan & Garcia Laborda, 2012; Peterson & Jabbari, 2023).

Educational games

Gamification ideas are used in educational games specifically created for language learning to make language acquisition interesting and successful. To accommodate a range of student demands, these games frequently include interactive features, flexible learning pathways, and real-time feedback. One of these games is Duolingo, a gamified platform that teaches vocabulary, grammar, listening, and pronunciation through brief lessons, interactive exercises, and prizes like points and streaks. Research has demonstrated that the gamification features and adaptive algorithms of Duolingo improve student motivation and retention (Gee & Gao, 2022). According to Bader et al. (2022), the gamification features on Duolingo, like progress bars, tests, and streak systems, affect user motivation and engagement. Potential disadvantages are also covered, such as cycles of disengagement and addictive behaviours. A mixed-methods study done by Kazu & Kuvvetli(2025) assessing Duolingo's efficacy in raising high school students' language proficiency assesses its impact on speaking, listening, reading, and writing abilities. The study uses a quasi-experimental methodology to assess how Duolingo's adaptive learning system affects different language proficiency levels.

An additional game is Quizlet, a flexible learning tool that is frequently used for vocabulary review and acquisition (Platzer, 2020). Although not solely for language learning, it has a number of features that are particularly helpful in this regard, such as customisable sets that let students learn new words and their definitions (Lukov, 2022). Additionally, interactive games such as 'Match' and 'Gravity' test students' ability to quickly remember definitions and words. Its 'Learn' function employs spaced repetition to concentrate on the terms that the student finds most difficult (Platzer, 2020). A community of shared resources can be fostered by teachers and students sharing flashcard sets. Reading words and sentences out loud helps with pronunciation practice. Dizon's (2016) analysis illustrates how Quizlet's features, like interactive testing and flashcards, greatly increase vocabulary engagement and retention. Lukov (2022) looked into how Quizlet affected students' acquisition of Academic Word List (AWL) vocabulary. He discovered that Quizlet greatly increased foreign students' language retention and knowledge. The study also looked at the function of pictures in flashcards and found that whereas pictures improved retention right away, they were less effective over the long run. Studies have indicated that mobile apps such as Quizlet improve vocabulary acquisition by fostering a more active and self-directed learning environment. Interactive Quizlet elements like game modes and flashcards have been shown to increase student motivation and retention (Lukov, 2022).

Commercial off-the-shelf games

Commercial off-the-shelf games (COTS) that have been modified for language instruction are another category of games. Because they provide learners with immersive and captivating environments, COTS digital games have been utilised for language instruction in and outside schools more and more (Al-Obaydi, Pikhart & Shakki, 2023; Sundqvist, 2019). Originally created for amusement, these games offer real-world language usage situations that promote cooperation, communication, and problem-solving.

One of these games is the sandbox game Minecraft, which has been utilised extensively in language teaching and learning because of its flexible features. It is a useful tool for language learning because players complete activities that call for reading, writing, and verbal communication. According to research, by involving players in interactive storytelling and group projects, Minecraft promotes vocabulary growth and contextual learning (Reinhardt & Thorne, 2020). The function of digital gaming in accidental second language (L2) acquisition is examined in the study by Al-Obaydi, Pikhart, and Shakki (2023), especially in the context of EFL (English as a Foreign Language). Their study focuses on how young learners' vocabulary acquisition and retention are aided by games like Among Us and Minecraft. The notion that commercial off-the-shelf (COTS) games can be beneficial for language instruction is supported by this study.

Another life-simulation game that lets users create and control people in different social situations is The Sims. Players are exposed to commonplace terminology, conversations, and decision-making processes in this game, which aids in language learning. Research shows that contextual interactions and story-driven gaming in The Sims improve English comprehension (Reinhardt & Sykes, 2014).

An additional multiplayer social deduction game is called Among Us, and in order to spot imposters, participants must be able to speak clearly. The game is an excellent resource for language learners because it relies on debate, argumentation, and logic. According to research, in language learning settings, Among Us promotes critical thinking, negotiation techniques, and conversational skills (Sundqvist, 2019).

The use of Player Unknown's Battlegrounds (PUBG) for language acquisition has also been investigated, especially in casual and immersive contexts. As a multiplayer battle royal game, PUBG requires players to employ language in real time while strategising, interacting with teammates, and responding to changing circumstances (Al-Obaydi et al., 2025; Pikhart et al., 2024; Tawafak et al., 2023). Research has looked into how PUBG affects language learning. PUBG had a mixed impact on language learning, according to one study, even though players were exposed to English (Julian, 2022). Another study emphasised the impact of PUBG's popularity on digital game-based language acquisition, stressing the value of contact and participation (Loughton, 2025). Language hunting in PUBG has also been studied by some educators, who have found helpful terms and expressions that players inadvertently learn while playing.

By offering learners engaging and dynamic experiences that improve their language skills, these games are prime examples of how COTS digital games may be used to teach languages.

Serious games

Serious games are made primarily to teach, train, or solve real-world problems rather than just for fun. They incorporate game features like challenges, prizes, and interactivity to keep users interested while teaching them useful skills, information, or mindsets (Mitsea et al., 2025). These games are used in a variety of contexts, including education, where their interactive scenarios and simulations help improve students' understanding of subjects like science, arithmetic, and history (Gundersen & Lampropoulos, 2025). They are also employed in healthcare since they may be used to train medical staff, educate patients, and promote healthy behaviours through games that are fitness and therapeutic in nature (Kara, 2021). According to Mitsea et al. (2025), digital simulations are widely utilised in corporate training to foster soft skills like leadership and teamwork through immersive, scenario-based experiences. These resources have social impact in addition to professional development goals by using gripping stories to increase public awareness and motivate action on urgent societal challenges (Gundersen & Lampropoulos, 2025).

The effectiveness of serious games and gamified language learning platforms for language acquisition differs significantly, according to experimental investigations comparing the two. One way to explain motivation and engagement is as the deeper engagement which is fostered by the engrossing tales and problem-solving settings that serious games offer. With gamified platforms, however, motivation is maintained through leaderboards, badges, and awards Yanes & Bououd, 2019). According to research, gamified platforms emphasise repeated practice and reinforcement, but serious games improve contextual language use and critical thinking (Chan & Lo, 2024). A systematic review conducted by Nilubol & Sitthitikul (2023), gamified platforms are better for short-term vocabulary learning, whereas serious games enhance long-term retention and authentic language application.

It's crucial to distinguish between gamified language learning platforms and serious games, especially in the field of educational technology and language acquisition studies. Comprehending this distinction can offer valuable perspectives on deep learning and cognitive engagement (Hamari et al., 2016), language transferability and retention (Reinhardt & Sykes, 2012), and Personalised Learning and Adaptability (de Freitas, 2018).

To sum up, gamified language learning platforms and serious games have unique benefits and meet various learning requirements. Deeper cognitive engagement, problem-solving abilities, and contextual language use are all enhanced by serious games, and these abilities can lead to authentic application and long-term memory. However, with features like leaderboards and prizes, gamified platforms offer powerful resources for short-term vocabulary learning, repetitive practice, and extrinsic incentive. Designing more successful language learning strategies that combine motivational frameworks with immersion to meet a variety of learner profiles and educational objectives requires an understanding of their differences and complementarities. When used carefully in the environment of language acquisition, both strategies have substantial benefits.

Table 5. Main types of digital games that are used to teach languages

Type of Digital Game	Description	Examples
Educational Games	Games that are specifically made to help people learn, with an emphasis on language abilities like grammar, pronunciation, and vocabulary.	Kahoot, Quizlet, and Duolingo
Commercial off-the-Shelf Games (COTS)	The immersive and participatory quality of games led to their adaptation for language learning even though they were not initially intended for instructional purposes.	Among Us, The Sims, and Minecraft
Serious Games	Real-world scenarios are frequently incorporated into games created for certain educational goals in order to provide context-based language instruction.	Mission US, Third World Farmer, Influent

Practical applications

Using digital games in the classroom can be a game-changer for improving student learning. Classrooms have effectively used MinecraftEdu to encourage creativity and teamwork. In the gaming environment, teachers have used it to create lessons where students construct historical landmarks or work out mathematical puzzles. This method promotes problem-solving abilities and teamwork (Marklund & Alklind, 2016). Prodigy and DragonBox are two examples of digital games that have been used into math classes to help students visualise abstract ideas. Students are drawn in by these games' dynamic challenges and rewards, which enable them to learn difficult concepts through play (Gros, 2015). Additionally, gamified features are incorporated into language learning games like Duolingo and Influent. They offer immersive experiences that allow students to practice grammar and vocabulary in authentic settings, which is consistent with ideas such as Krashen's Input Hypothesis ((Bailey & Fahad, 2021; Gros, 2015). Teaching historical things and urban planning has been done through strategy games like Civilisation and SimCity. Through the use of historical events or urban development scenarios, these games force students to make decisions, which develops their critical thinking and decision-making abilities. Students can also investigate scientific ideas like physics and biochemistry through games like Foldit and Kerbal Space Program. These games offer chances for practical experimentation, making difficult scientific concepts interesting and approachable (Gros, 2015).

Frameworks for lesson plans that incorporate games for particular language skills are creative ways to combine interactive learning with teaching. These frameworks use the captivating and immersive qualities of games to improve language acquisition. For instance, vocabulary-building games like Word Association or Scrabble push students to investigate and use new terms in context, whereas audio-based tests or games that focus on listening comprehension, like Simon Says, aim to enhance auditory skills. By encouraging fluency and confidence in communicating, role-playing or discussion games can enhance speaking practice (TESOL International Association; SlideShare). Lesson plans that incorporate games are in line with theories such as Krashen's Input Hypothesis, which highlights the significance of understandable input in language acquisition. Additionally, by encouraging active engagement and practical language use, gamified approaches align with the tenets of Communicative Language Teaching. Resources like TeachingEnglish and My English Pages offer comprehensive advice on how to organise lessons using games. These sites offer examples and concepts that are specific to language teaching situations (Cambridge English; TESOL International Association).

There are case studies and success stories that demonstrate how digital games can be used into classroom instruction. For example, Matić & Abrantes Garcêz Palha (2023) looked at how a teacher used the game Probchallenge to improve student learning. The results showed that although digital games can be useful, attaining learning goals depends heavily on teachers' comprehension of game-based pedagogy. Vu and Feinstein (2017) have another one that is an experimental study looked into how game-based learning was used in various STEM courses. The findings indicated that integrating digital games into the classroom led to favourable behavioural changes and enhanced problem-solving abilities among the pupils.

As long as they are used carefully and in line with educational objectives, these examples show how digital games can improve learning outcomes. Digital games may encourage motivation, engagement, and deeper learning when they are thoughtfully included into the classroom. Games can be effective facilitators of critical thinking, teamwork, and problem-solving when they are in line with educational frameworks.

Challenges and future considerations

Digital games present fascinating opportunities for teaching languages, but there are drawbacks and things to keep in mind. With their immersive and interactive features, digital games have the potential to significantly improve language acquisition. Nonetheless, educators and researchers must address the difficulties and factors that come with using them in educational settings. For instance, it takes careful selection to integrate games into curricula while guaranteeing compatibility with language learning theories like CLT, as not all games are made with education in mind (Law et al., 2008; Reinders & Wattana, 2015).

Evaluation challenges are another issue. Innovative methods that complement the dynamic and interactive nature of games are needed for assessment and measurement of learning objectives in contexts involving games (Kim & Ifenthaler, 2019). The level of learning in these settings might not be adequately captured by conventional evaluation techniques like tests or quizzes. Instead, strategies like stealth assessment, in which evaluation is smoothly incorporated into games, are being utilised more and more to track abilities like teamwork, critical thinking, and problem-solving in real time (Shute et al., 2017). These tests provide a customised learning experience by giving quick feedback and adjusting to the learner's development (Burmich et al., 2023). To make it possible to ensure that evaluations appropriately represent the desired learning outcomes, research highlights the significance of matching game objectives with educational goals

(Kim & Ifenthaler, 2019). Evaluating learning results might be difficult since traditional tests might not accurately gauge language proficiency gained through gaming (Darin et al., 2023).

Accessibility and technology concerns were also brought up since certain students might not have access to the hardware, dependable internet connections, or digital literacy abilities needed for productive participation (Peterson, 2010). Lack of access to computers, cellphones, and tablets, especially in low-income or rural areas, is one technological impediment to the use of digital games in education. Unreliable or nonexistent internet connectivity exacerbates this problem by making it difficult to play online games (Patagar et al., 2023). A financial barrier may also be created by the price of gadgets, software, and internet services, which may be unaffordable for many. Even when these materials are available, their efficient use may be hampered by teachers' and students' lack of digital literacy. In order to provide fair access to digital games for education, these obstacles highlight the necessity of better infrastructure, reasonably priced solutions, and focused digital skills training (Patagar et al., 2023). On the other hand, teacher integration and training provide significant challenges. Professional development is necessary for the successful application of game-based learning approaches, as many educators lack familiarity with them ((Avidov-Ungar & Hayak, 2023; Gee, 2003). Furthermore, cognitive load and distraction are also addressed in this concern. While games can be entertaining, poorly designed ones may detract from language learning objectives rather than support it (Reinders & Wattana, 2015).

Certain considerations, such game design and selection, should also be properly taken into account. It's critical to select games that support active language use and correspond with learning objectives (Ishaq et al., 2022). Second, finding a balance between enjoyment and education. The most successful games guarantee motivation without sacrificing instructional value by fusing interest with well-defined learning objectives (Natucci & Borges, 2023). Collaborative and social language acquisition can be improved by learning through games that encourage peer engagement, teamwork, and real-time communication (Adipat et al., 2021). Language and cultural appropriateness are also crucial. To ensure inclusion and relevance, games should be able to be adjusted to a variety of learner backgrounds (Ishaq et al., 2022). Lastly, long-term implementation and scalability. Institutional support, continuous research, and technological flexibility are necessary for successful integration (Natucci & Borges, 2023).

For the purpose of retaining student motivation while accomplishing pedagogical goals, digital games for English instruction must integrate engaging gameplay mechanics with educational content in order to balance entertainment and learning objectives (Pikhart et al., 2024b). In order to engage students, effective games integrate language activities like vocabulary development, grammar drills, and conversation practice with stories, obstacles, and rewards. This method guarantees that students stay engrossed in the game while improving their linguistic abilities (Adipat et al., 2021). According to research, well-made games can boost motivation, lower anxiety, and encourage active engagement, making them effective language learning aids (Ali et al., 2023; Pikhart et al., 2024b; Xu et al., 2020).

The use of digital games in language instruction gives tremendous chances for engagement, motivation, and learning, but it also comes with problems. Issues such as technological accessibility, digital literacy, and alignment with pedagogical goals might limit its effective application. Furthermore, creative approaches that go beyond conventional techniques are needed to evaluate learning outcomes in game-based environments. Notwithstanding these challenges, digital games have the potential to be an effective tool for contemporary language instruction since they can encourage motivation, teamwork, and, when appropriately incorporated, immersion language practice.

Possible future trends

Technological developments, pedagogical breakthroughs, and growing awareness of game-based learning as a powerful teaching tool will all influence the use of digital games in language instruction in the future. A number of significant trends are developing, including AI integration and adaptive learning. According to Nilubol & Sitthitikul, (2023), the increasingly complex AI-powered games provide individualised learning experiences that adapt to the skill levels of each learner. By analysing player interactions and offering customised feedback, these systems improve efficacy and engagement. Additionally, gamification in language learning platforms refers to the growing use of gamification features, like leaderboards, badges, and awards, in language learning programs. These characteristics increase motivation and promote consistent participation in language learning activities (Thurairasu, 2022).

An additional trend is the use of immersive technologies (VR & AR) into language learning games. According to Aprea & Ifenthaler (2021), these technologies offer immersive environments that allow learners to develop real-world communication abilities in virtual scenarios. These technological advancements promote retention and contextual learning. Another trend is multiplayer and social learning. Peer contact and target language communication are being promoted by cooperative learning environments and online multiplayer games. By promoting social interaction and genuine language use, these platforms enhance the dynamic and interactive nature of learning (Aprea & Ifenthaler, 2021).

Both micro learning and mobile methods are the current trends in which mobile-friendly language games are becoming more and more popular, enabling students to participate in brief, targeted learning sessions (Thurairasu, 2022). The students can fit these short tasks into their hectic schedule and practice their language skills consistently. As more educational institutions realise the potential of digital games to improve language learning, they have begun to integrate them into their curricula (Nilubol & Sitthitikul, 2023). To match educational standards with game-based learning, frameworks supported by research are being developed.

The unique ways that new tools like AI tutors, adaptive learning platforms, and digital games transform language learning processes must be highlighted, even while the wider educational consequences of digitalisation are noteworthy. Through self-paced learning and tailored feedback, these technologies increase learner autonomy. They also improve affective engagement by lowering fear and boosting motivation, and they facilitate communicative competence through immersive, interaction-rich settings. These affordances make digital instruments dynamic facilitators of language development rather than just teaching tools.

According to these tendencies, digital games will keep developing into effective teaching aids for languages since they provide immersive, dynamic, and captivating learning environments. The use of digital games in language instruction has a bright future because to developments in artificial intelligence (AI), immersive technologies like virtual reality (VR) and augmented reality (AR), and the gamification of educational platforms (Nilubol & Sitthitikul, 2023). These developments promise tailored, flexible learning experiences that will improve language acquisition and increase student engagement. Furthermore, the growing use of social and multiplayer learning games encourages genuine student cooperation and communication (Aprea & Ifenthaler, 2021). Digital games have the potential to revolutionise language instruction by bridging the gap between pedagogy and enjoyment and meeting the demands of a wide range of learners as they become more integrated with formal education.

Conclusion

The use of digital games in language instruction is indicative of a move toward learner-centred methods (Xu et al., 2020). Because digital games encourage active participation, autonomy, and individualised learning experiences, they complement learner-centred approaches in language learning (Al-Obaydi, Pikart &

Klimova, 2023). They motivate students to take an active role in their education by resolving issues and making choices immediately (Pikhart et al., 2024b). The tenets of learner-centred approaches, which prioritise active engagement, are consistent with this (Tawafak et al., 2025).

Based on the thematic analysis of the present chapter, it is clear that games offer chances for genuine communication, teamwork, and problem-solving, all of which are in line with contemporary educational objectives. Personalised experiences that meet the demands of different language learners are made possible by the application of AI and adaptive learning systems (Adipat et al., 2021). By creating realistic environments for language practice, immersive technologies like VR and AR help close the gap between theory and practice (Aprea & Ifenthaler, 2021). The digital gap is still a major barrier, though, as differences in device and internet connectivity availability restrict the application of these advancements. Teachers are also faced with difficulties due to the absence of defined frameworks for incorporating games into courses. Screen time and data privacy are two ethical issues that need to be carefully considered (Avidov-Ungar & Hayak, 2023).

A more methodical integration of language-specific pedagogical difficulties, such as vocabulary acquisition, pronunciation help, and intercultural communication, has been emphasised in order to increase the book's applicability to language educators. These aspects show the special affordances of developing technologies in meeting the complex requirements of digital language acquisition, in addition to reflecting those demands. The book seeks to provide a more focused and useful framework for practitioners navigating the changing landscape of language teaching by placing these opportunities within larger digital trends.

According to the available literature, digital games have shown themselves to be revolutionary resources for language learning, providing a special fusion of teaching and engagement. Constructivism and Krashen's Input Hypothesis are two theoretical underpinnings that support the use of games as settings for meaningful input and active learning (Xu et al., 2020). The growing use of gamification, artificial intelligence, and immersive technologies like virtual reality and augmented reality, which improve contextual learning and personalisation, is highlighted by research trends in this chapter. Their usefulness in enhancing speaking, hearing, and vocabulary while boosting motivation and lowering fear is demonstrated by real-world applications (Al-Obaydi, Pikhart & Shakki, 2023). Nonetheless, issues including gaps in digital literacy, technological hurdles, and the requirement for creative evaluation techniques continue to exist. To fully realise the promise of digital games in language instruction, these issues must be resolved.

Teachers are crucial because they will have a significant impact on how language learning develops in the future, and digital games offer a potent chance to turn conventional teaching strategies into fun, interactive experiences (Avidov-Ungar & Hayak, 2023). Innovative, game-based tactics that improve motivation, encourage teamwork, and offer real-world language practice are at the heart of a call to action for educators to embrace digital games (Aprea & Ifenthaler, 2021). These games foster vocabulary acquisition, grammatical comprehension, and conversational skills while lowering learning anxiety by allowing students to interact with language in relevant, contextualised contexts (Al-Aosail et al., 2024). By integrating digital games into their instructional strategies, teachers may close the gap between pedagogy and entertainment, guaranteeing dynamic and engaging language learning (Chen & Tu, 2021). AI-powered gamification and personalisation strategies allow for customised learning experiences that efficiently advance students at various skill levels (Nilubol & Sitthitikul, 2023). Furthermore, peer communication and interaction are promoted by multiplayer games, which makes language learning a social and interactive activity. Teachers should investigate existing studies, try out game-based teaching, study the time invested, and promote the inclusion of digital tools in curriculum for the purpose of fully realise the potential of digital games (Al-Obaydi et al., 2025). They can adapt game-based approaches to meet the requirements of a variety of learners with the support of collaborative teaching communities and professional development programmes (Avidov-Ungar & Hayak, 2023). As digital literacy develops further, using digital games as teaching aids is becoming essential to improving the effectiveness, adaptability, and engagement of language training. Interactive interactions and multimodal texts are two ways that digital games support literacy instruction (Alahmari et al., 2023). They draw attention to how games blend narratives, graphics, and gameplay elements, making them excellent teaching tools for critical reading and analysis. Games, as opposed to texts, encourage students to learn actively and collaboratively while developing their ability to make decisions and solve problems.

The theme-based review of earlier research made in this chapter concludes by highlighting the revolutionary potential of digital games in learning environments, especially in language instruction. Recurring themes are highlighted, including how gamification can improve student engagement and how game-based systems can be tailored to meet the demands of different users. There are still gaps in areas like teacher preparedness, accessibility, and cultural sensitivity, though, which suggests that more research is needed. By combining these ideas, the chapter advances our knowledge of how digital games affect learning outcomes and opens the door for future studies and well-informed implementations.

Recommendations and implications

The main recommendation remarks focus on increasing infrastructure and accessibility is a top goal in order to guarantee the effective integration of digital games into language instruction. Many students, particularly those in underprivileged communities, encounter obstacles including inconsistent internet connectivity and restricted gadget access. Broadband infrastructure should be improved, gadgets should be made more inexpensive or subsidised, and governments and educational institutions should make investments to increase access to technology. Programs like mobile-friendly game adaptations and technology lending can help close the digital divide and provide equal chances for all students. The successful adoption of game-based learning depends on providing educators with the required professional development and training. To effectively use digital games in the classroom, educators must possess a solid grasp of pedagogy, evaluation techniques, and game mechanics. The main goals of thorough training programmes should be to incorporate games into the curriculum, provide captivating learning environments, and monitor student progress with data-driven insights. Maximising the potential of digital games for language learning will be made easier for teachers by offering workshops, certifications, and chances for ongoing professional development.

Innovative strategies that go beyond conventional testing techniques are needed to evaluate learning outcomes in game-based environments. Alternative approaches like in-game analytics, real-time feedback systems, and stealth assessments are necessary since traditional evaluations frequently fall short of capturing the entire spectrum of skills acquired via gameplay. By using these techniques, teachers may easily keep an eye on their students' progress without interfering with the immersive learning process. It is important to create frameworks that are informed by research to make sure that evaluation is in line with educational goals. In order to strengthen educational value and student motivation, such frameworks must carefully balance the demanding character of game-based learning with the rigour of instruction.

Digital games for language learning will be further improved by promoting multidisciplinary research and development. More successful and captivating game-based learning environments can be produced through cooperation between linguists, educators, game designers, and technologists. The effects of immersive technology, gamification techniques, and AI-driven personalisation on language learning should all be investigated in research projects. To determine the long-term efficacy of digital games in promoting language proficiency across various learner groups, longitudinal research has to be carried out.

For digital games to be widely adopted, it is imperative that they conform to formal education requirements. Curriculum designers and educational policymakers should endeavour to incorporate game-based learning into current frameworks so that language learning games enhance rather than replace conventional teaching techniques. Teachers can develop a well-rounded strategy that uses both digital and conventional teaching techniques to improve learning objectives and student involvement by creating structured lesson plans that include digital games.

To guarantee that digital games are used responsibly in language instruction, ethical issues must also be taken into account. Prioritising well-being, data privacy, and inclusion can help developers and educators create games that meet the needs of a wide range of learners while protecting user privacy. Techniques for limiting excessive screen usage and encouraging a good balance between online and offline learning should be put into place. Establishing clear rules is necessary to build digital learning settings that are both ethical and safe.

Lastly, utilising cutting-edge technology like AI, VR, and AR can completely transform language instruction. Adaptive learning driven by AI may tailor experiences according to each learner's degree of skill, while immersive technologies offer authentic language practice situations. These developments will improve engagement, promote deeper learning, and present creative chances for interactive and hands-on language learning when incorporated into game-based learning. By following these recommendations, stakeholders may overcome current obstacles and optimise the potential of digital games to revolutionise language instruction.

parents must work together to set reasonable limits on screen time and encourage activities that promote physical and mental well-being. The screen time should not be extended for non-serious reasons, and the technologies should not be used in situations where they can be used, but only where they must be used because of the very clear added value. Moreover, the internet is a vast resource, but it also contains content that may be inappropriate or harmful to younger adults. Educators should implement content filters and provide guidance on safe internet practices to protect students from exposure to harmful material.

Among other serious threats caused by digital technologies are social isolation and addiction. Digital technologies can easily lead to social isolation and serious addiction, particularly when students spend excessive time online at the expense of face-to-face interactions, meaningful activities and social contacts. It is important to promote a healthy and sensible approach to technology use, encouraging students to engage in offline activities as much as possible, such as physical activity, social encounters, playing an instrument, reading books, and, mainly, building meaningful emotional relationships.

It is important to say that there ought to be strategies for promoting digital literacy and healthy screen habits (Pikhart et al., 2023). Educators can play a crucial role in creating and promoting these strategies. This includes teaching students how to use digital tools responsibly, critically evaluating online information (if it is possible at all), and developing time management skills to balance screen time with other activities.

The rise of AI

The advent of AI in education introduces a new set of ethical dilemmas and possible serious challenges (Pikhart et al., 2024). On the positive note, AI technologies can personalise learning experiences and provide valuable insights, but they can also pose risks related to addiction, social isolation, data privacy, accountability and probably other serious threats we are now aware of. The absolute lack of comprehensive data on the short- and long-term impacts of AI in education calls for cautious and restrained implementation. Researchers and educators, not politicians and corporations, must collaborate to explore these ethical issues and develop guidelines to ensure AI is used responsibly in educational settings.

AI has the potential to revolutionise education by providing personalised learning experiences, automating administrative tasks, and offering real-time feedback, all these aspects are extremely positive. However, these benefits come with risks, including the potential for bias in AI algorithms, the erosion of privacy, and the lack of transparency in AI decision-making processes. Moreover, the subjective personal risks, such as addiction and social isolation, are not revealed yet (Pikhart & Al-Obaydi, 2023).

One of the major problems is that AI systems often rely on large datasets, raising concerns about data privacy and security. Additionally, it is essential to ensure that AI systems are designed and implemented with fairness and accountability in mind, with mechanisms in place to address any ethical issues that arise. The long-term impacts of AI in education are not yet fully understood, and there is a need for ongoing research to explore these effects. Educators and policymakers should adopt a cautious approach to AI implementation, prioritising ethical considerations and seeking to understand the potential consequences before widespread adoption (Pikhart & Al-Obaydi, 2023).

Call for ethical restraint and further research

Given the potential ethical pitfalls, it is imperative to exercise restraint in the widespread adoption of AI and other digital technologies in education. It is necessary to advocate for a balanced approach, emphasising the need for ongoing research to understand the ethical implications fully. By prioritising ethical considerations, we can harness the benefits of digital technologies while safeguarding the integrity and well-being of learners. Continuous research is essential to identify and address emerging ethical issues in digital education. This includes studying the long-term impacts of digital tools on students' mental health, social development, and academic outcomes.

Following the research findings, clear guidelines and best practices are needed to ensure the responsible use of AI in education. This includes establishing ethical standards for data privacy, fairness, and accountability, as well as providing training for educators on the ethical use of AI technologies. While digital technologies offer significant benefits, it is crucial to balance these advantages with ethical considerations. By adopting a thoughtful and measured approach, we can maximise the positive impact of digital tools while minimising potential harms.

As digital technologies become increasingly integrated into educational environments, the importance of ethical awareness cannot be overstated. It is important to realise that educators, policymakers, and stakeholders must address ethical considerations to ensure the responsible use of digital tools in education.

Data privacy and security

One of the foremost ethical concerns in digital education is the protection of students' personal information. Digital tools often collect and store vast amounts of data, making it essential to implement robust security measures to prevent unauthorised access and data breaches. Educators and institutions must be transparent about data collection practices and ensure compliance with privacy regulations (Klimova et al., 2023).

Students and educators should be fully informed about what data is being collected, how it will be used, and who will have access to it. Obtaining explicit consent is crucial to maintaining trust and ensuring ethical data practices.

Implementing strong security protocols, such as encryption and regular security audits, can help safeguard sensitive information. Institutions should also provide training for educators and staff on data security best practices. Educators should focus on promoting digital literacy, equipping students with the skills needed to navigate and utilise digital tools effectively. This includes teaching students how to critically evaluate online information and use technology responsibly.

Responsible use of digital tools

The integration of digital tools in education should be guided by ethical principles that prioritise the well-being of students. This includes selecting age-appropriate content that is suitable for the developmental stage of the learners. While digital tools offer numerous benefits, it is important to balance their use with traditional teaching methods. This ensures that students develop a well-rounded skill set and are not overly reliant on technology. Digital tools should be used to enhance critical thinking and problem-solving skills. Educators can leverage technology to create interactive and engaging learning experiences that challenge students to think deeply and creatively.

Educators should receive ongoing professional development to stay informed about the latest ethical issues in digital education. This includes training on data privacy, security, inclusivity, and responsible use of digital tools. Educators must be equipped to make ethical decisions regarding the use of digital technologies in their classrooms. This involves considering the potential impacts on students' well-being and ensuring that technology is used to support, rather than hinder, learning. Ethical awareness in digital education requires collaboration among educators, administrators, policymakers, and technology developers. By working together, stakeholders can develop comprehensive guidelines and best practices to ensure the responsible use of digital tools.

Ethical awareness is a critical component of digital education. By addressing key ethical considerations, such as data privacy, inclusivity, and responsible use of digital tools, educators can create a safe and supportive learning environment for all students. This chapter highlights the importance of ongoing professional development and collaborative efforts to ensure that digital technologies are used ethically and effectively in education.

Ethical issues in foreign language learning

Foreign language education, facilitated by digital technologies, offers unique opportunities for cultural exchange and global communication (Klimova & Pikhart, 2025). However, it also presents distinct ethical challenges that educators must navigate to ensure respectful and inclusive learning experiences. This chapter delves into the ethical issues specific to foreign language learning and provides suggested strategies for addressing them.

Digital language learning tools often include content that reflects specific cultural perspectives. It is essential to ensure that these tools represent diverse cultures accurately and respectfully. Educators should critically evaluate digital resources to avoid perpetuating stereotypes or biases and strive to provide a balanced and inclusive view of different cultures.

Educators must be vigilant in selecting digital content that portrays cultures in a nuanced and respectful manner. This involves choosing resources that highlight the diversity within cultures and avoid oversimplified or biased representations. Teaching foreign languages involves more than just linguistic skills; it includes fostering cultural sensitivity and understanding. Educators should use digital tools to promote cultural awareness and encourage students to appreciate and respect cultural differences. Not all digital resources are reliable or accurate. Educators should critically assess (if possible at all) the quality of digital tools and materials, ensuring they provide accurate and valuable information. This includes verifying the credibility of sources and avoiding resources that may contain misinformation, having in mind how difficult, or even impossible, task this can be (Klimova et al., 2023).

Students should be taught to conduct research ethically, using digital tools responsibly. This includes understanding how to cite sources correctly, avoiding plagiarism, and respecting the intellectual property of others. Language learning involves communication, and digital tools can facilitate interactions between students from different cultural backgrounds. Educators should emphasise the importance of ethical communication practices, such as respecting cultural differences, avoiding offensive language, and promoting positive and constructive interactions. Teaching students digital etiquette is crucial for fostering respectful online communication. This includes guidelines on how to interact politely, avoid cyberbullying, and maintain a positive online presence. Digital tools can be used to connect students with peers from other countries, providing opportunities for intercultural exchange. Educators should guide students in these interactions, helping them develop intercultural competence and understanding.

Impact on younger adults

The integration of digital technologies in education has profound implications for younger adults. While these tools offer numerous benefits, they also present significant ethical challenges that must be addressed to ensure the well-being of students. This chapter explores the impact of digital technologies on younger adults, focusing on issues related to screen time, exposure to harmful content, social isolation, addiction, and strategies for promoting digital literacy and healthy screen habits (Pikhart & Al-Obaydi, 2023).

Excessive screen time can have adverse effects on mental health, including increased anxiety, depression, and sleep disturbances. Younger adults are particularly vulnerable to these impacts, as they may spend significant amounts of time on digital devices for both educational and recreational purposes. Educators and parents must work together to set reasonable limits on screen time and encourage activities that promote physical and mental well-being. This includes incorporating breaks during digital learning sessions and promoting offline activities that foster social interaction and physical exercise. Schools and educational institutions should provide resources and support for students experiencing mental health issues related to screen time. This includes access to counselling services and educational programmes that promote mental health awareness.

The internet is a vast resource, but it also contains content that may be inappropriate or harmful to younger adults. Educators should implement content filters and provide guidance on safe internet practices to protect students from exposure to harmful material. Teaching students about digital literacy is crucial for helping them navigate the internet safely. This includes educating them on how to identify and avoid harmful content, understand privacy settings, and report inappropriate material. Parents play a key role in monitoring and guiding their children's internet use. Educators should collaborate with parents to provide resources and strategies for ensuring safe and responsible internet use at home.

Digital technologies can lead to social isolation, particularly when students spend excessive time online at the expense of face-to-face interactions. This can impact their social skills and overall well-being. It is important to promote a balanced approach to technology use, encouraging students to engage in offline activities and build meaningful relationships. Schools can organise social events and activities that foster in-person interactions and community building. Digital addiction is a growing concern, with younger adults at risk of becoming overly dependent on digital devices. Educators should be aware of the signs of digital addiction and provide support and resources to help students manage their technology use.

Schools should implement comprehensive digital literacy programmes that equip students with the skills needed to use digital tools responsibly. This includes teaching students how to critically evaluate online information, understand digital ethics, and develop time management skills. Educators can play a crucial role in promoting healthy screen habits. This includes setting guidelines for screen time, encouraging regular breaks, and promoting activities that balance digital and offline experiences. Promoting digital literacy and healthy screen habits requires collaboration among educators, parents, and students. By working together, stakeholders can create a supportive environment that fosters responsible technology use.

The rise of the implementation of AI in education

Artificial Intelligence (AI) is revolutionising various sectors, including education. While AI technologies offer significant potential to enhance learning experiences, they also introduce new ethical dilemmas. This chapter explores the benefits and risks of AI in education, focusing on issues related to privacy, fairness, accountability, and the need for cautious implementation (Reiss, 2021).

AI has the potential to tailor educational content to individual students' needs, providing personalised learning experiences that can improve engagement and outcomes. AI-driven tools can adapt to students' learning styles, pace, and preferences, offering customised support and feedback. AI can streamline administrative tasks, such as grading and scheduling, allowing educators to focus more on teaching and student interaction. This can lead to increased efficiency and reduced workload for teachers. AI technologies can provide real-time feedback to students, helping them identify areas for improvement and track their progress. This immediate feedback can enhance the learning process and support continuous development.

Despite its benefits, AI also poses significant risks. These include potential biases in AI algorithms, privacy concerns related to data collection, and the lack of transparency in AI decision-making processes. It is crucial to address these risks to ensure that AI technologies are used ethically and effectively. AI systems often rely on large datasets, raising concerns about data privacy and security. It is essential to implement robust measures to protect students' personal information and ensure compliance with privacy regulations. Transparency about data collection practices and obtaining explicit consent are critical to maintaining trust. AI algorithms can inadvertently perpetuate biases present in the data they are trained on, leading to unfair outcomes. Educators and developers must critically evaluate AI tools to identify and mitigate biases, ensuring that AI technologies promote fairness and inclusivity. The use of AI in education should be transparent, with clear explanations of how AI algorithms work and what data they use. Developers and educators must advocate for accountability in AI development, ensuring that ethical standards are upheld and that there are mechanisms in place to address any ethical issues that arise.

The long-term impacts of AI in education are not yet fully understood, and there is a need for ongoing research to explore these effects. This includes studying the potential consequences of AI on students' learning, mental health, and social development. Given the uncertainties surrounding AI, it is important to adopt a cautious approach to its implementation in education. This involves piloting AI technologies in controlled settings, gathering data on their impacts, and making informed decisions based on evidence. Researchers, educators, and policymakers must collaborate to explore the ethical implications of AI in education. By working together, stakeholders can develop guidelines and best practices to ensure the responsible use of AI technologies (Luckin, 2023).

Clear ethical standards and guidelines are needed to govern the use of AI in education. This includes establishing principles for data privacy, fairness, and accountability, as well as providing training for educators on the ethical use of AI technologies. Developers should prioritise ethical considerations in the design and implementation of AI tools. This includes conducting thorough testing to identify and mitigate biases, ensuring transparency in AI decision-making processes, and engaging with educators to understand their needs and concerns. The primary goal of AI in education should be to enhance student well-being and learning outcomes. This involves using AI technologies to support, rather than replace, human interaction and instruction, and ensuring that AI tools are used in ways that promote positive educational experiences.

Call for ethical restraint and further research

As digital technologies and AI continue to evolve, their integration into education presents both opportunities and challenges. While these tools offer significant benefits, they also pose ethical dilemmas that require careful consideration. This chapter advocates for ethical restraint in the adoption of digital technologies, particularly AI, in education. It emphasises the need for ongoing research to fully understand the ethical implications and develop guidelines for responsible use.

Continuous research is essential to identify and address emerging ethical issues in digital education. This includes studying the long-term impacts of digital tools on students' mental health, social development, and academic outcomes. Researchers must investigate how these technologies affect different age groups, socio-economic backgrounds, and learning environments. Ethical research in digital education requires collaboration among various disciplines, including education, psychology, sociology, and computer science. By working together, researchers can gain a comprehensive understanding of the ethical challenges and develop holistic solutions. Educators and policymakers should base their decisions on robust research findings. This involves collecting and analysing data on the use of digital technologies in education, identifying best practices, and making informed choices that prioritise ethical considerations.

Clear guidelines and best practices are needed to ensure the responsible use of AI in education. This includes establishing ethical standards for data privacy, fairness, and accountability. Educators and developers should work together to create frameworks that govern the ethical use of AI technologies. Educators must receive training on the ethical use of AI and digital tools. This includes understanding the potential risks and benefits, learning how to critically evaluate AI technologies, and developing strategies to mitigate ethical issues. Ongoing professional development can help educators stay informed about the latest ethical challenges and solutions. Ethical guidelines should be developed through a collaborative process that involves educators, students, parents, policymakers, and technology developers. By engaging all stakeholders, the guidelines can reflect diverse perspectives and address the needs and concerns of the educational community.

Future directions for research and practice

Future research should focus on key areas such as the long-term impacts of AI on education, the effectiveness of digital literacy programmes, and the ethical challenges of emerging technologies. Researchers should prioritise studies that address the most pressing ethical issues and provide actionable insights. Researchers and developers should work together to create innovative solutions that address ethical challenges in digital education. This includes designing AI technologies that promote fairness and inclusivity, developing tools that enhance data privacy, and creating educational programmes that foster ethical awareness. Policymakers should advocate for ethical policies that govern the use of digital technologies in education. This includes establishing regulations that protect students' rights, promote inclusivity, and ensure accountability.

By implementing ethical policies, policymakers can create a supportive environment for responsible technology use.

The integration of digital technologies and AI in education presents significant ethical challenges that require careful consideration. By advocating for ethical restraint and emphasising the importance of ongoing research, educators and policymakers can ensure the responsible use of these tools. This chapter highlights the need for developing guidelines, promoting ethical awareness, and balancing benefits with ethical considerations. By prioritising ethical issues, we can harness the potential of digital technologies while safeguarding the integrity and well-being of learners.

Conclusion

Throughout this book chapter, we have explored the ethical considerations in digital technologies in foreign language education. We began by emphasising the importance of ethical awareness in digital education, highlighting key issues such as data privacy, security, inclusivity, and the digital divide. We then delved into the unique ethical challenges in foreign language learning, including cultural representation, intellectual property, and ethical communication practices. We examined the impact of digital technologies on younger adults, focusing on screen time, exposure to harmful content, social isolation, and addiction. Strategies for promoting digital literacy and healthy screen habits were discussed to mitigate these risks. The rise of AI in education was analysed, with a focus on the benefits and risks, privacy, fairness, accountability, and the need for cautious implementation. Finally, we advocated for ethical restraint in the adoption of digital technologies, particularly AI, in education. The importance of ongoing research, developing guidelines for responsible use, and balancing benefits with ethical considerations were emphasised.

The integration of digital technologies and AI in education offers significant opportunities to enhance learning experiences and outcomes. However, it also presents ethical dilemmas that must be carefully navigated. By prioritising ethical considerations, promoting ongoing research, and developing guidelines for responsible use, we can create a balanced and supportive educational environment. This chapter calls for a thoughtful and measured approach to the adoption of digital technologies, ensuring that they are used to benefit students while minimising potential harms.

CHAPTER 6

The new era of AI: Educational utilisation and future vision

Introduction

This chapter highlights the uses and promise of artificial intelligence (AI) tools, including ChatGPT, Copilot, DeepSeek, Gemini, Grok, and Perplexity, and examines how they can revolutionise education. A qualitative research method using thematic analysis is utilised in this chapter to combine themes and recurrent patterns from earlier studies on AI applications in language education settings. The findings show how these AI applications improve multimedia integration of language teaching and learning, expedite instructional operations, and support individualised learning. Furthermore, the chapter explores ethical issues, highlighting privacy, bias, and openness while discussing the difficulties in striking a balance between innovation and human-centred methods. According to future educational AI visions, adaptive learning technologies, immersive surroundings, and worldwide accessibility will all advance. The theoretical underpinnings and real-world applications are combined in this chapter to offer a thorough framework for comprehending and utilising AI's potential to transform language teaching and learning methods.

By increasing accessibility, automating administrative duties, and fostering individualised learning, AI is transforming education. Traditional educational methods are changing as a result of AI-driven technologies such as intelligent tutoring programs, adaptive learning platforms, and automated grading systems. By allowing teachers to adapt their lessons to each student's needs, these technologies increase student engagement and enhance learning results (Jain et al., 2025).

The potential of AI to deliver real-time assessment and feedback is one of its most important effects on education. Automated grading systems assess student's work in real time and provide helpful criticism to help students get better. AI-powered intelligent tutoring systems mimic human interactions by providing students with individualised explanations and guidance through challenging subjects. These developments keep instruction at a high level while lessening the workload for teachers (Javvaji & Veera Raghavulu, 2025).

AI is essential for improving accessibility in education as well. Assistive technologies, translation tools, and speech-to-text apps enable students with impairments get over obstacles to learning (Zdravkova, 2022). In order to ensure inclusion and fair access to education, AI-powered platforms can modify information to accommodate various learning styles and preferences (Pikhart et al., 2024). Furthermore, AI-powered analytics help organisations see learning patterns so that data-driven choices may be made about curriculum development and student assistance (Treve, 2025).

Notwithstanding its advantages, there are drawbacks to AI in education, such as worries about algorithmic bias, data privacy, and fair access (Kohnke et al., 2023). Despite its potential to boost language acquisition, particularly in terms of motivation and engagement, ChatGPT does not always result in instant behavioural improvements (Ali et al., 2023; Al-Obaydi et al., 2023). The massive gathering of student data presents moral dilemmas with regard to consent and security. Fairness in educational outcomes may also be impacted if AI models unintentionally perpetuate cultural biases seen in training data (Farrokhnia et al., 2024). To address these issues, ethical standards and open AI rules are necessary to guarantee responsible application (Jain et al., 2025).

The incorporation of artificial intelligence (AI)-driven applications like DeepSeek, ChatGPT, Perplexity, Copilot, Gemini, and Grok into educational settings has fundamentally changed teaching approaches. These technologies improve individualised instruction, streamline administrative duties, and offer immediate support, increasing the effectiveness and accessibility of education (Rahman et al., 2025). Platforms powered by AI provide adaptive learning by customising information to meet the needs of each individual learner, increasing comprehension and engagement (Macinska & Vinkler, 2024). ChatGPT and Copilot, for example, are popular tools for helping with coding and creating content. Because ChatGPT is so good at natural language processing, students may participate in engaging conversations and get prompt answers to their questions. Conversely, Copilot facilitates programming education by providing in-the-moment code recommendations and debugging guidance, which expedites the learning process for prospective developers (Rossettini et al., 2024). For students and teachers dealing with big datasets and challenging problem-solving situations, DeepSeek is a priceless tool because of its expertise in data analysis and scientific research (Rahman et al., 2025). Across the integration of text, graphics, and audio, Gemini and Grok enhance comprehension across a variety of media, contributing to multimodal learning experiences (Majeed et al., 2025). Grok is perfect for dynamic learning environments like stock market simulations or autonomous systems training because of its real-time data processing capabilities, while Gemini's capacity to process many data formats enables students to interact with content in a more comprehensive way. The uses of ChatGPT, DeepSeek, and Grok in language instruction are examined in Majeed et al. (2025), along with some of their advantages and disadvantages. Perplexity, renowned for its accuracy-focused search features, supports scholarly study by offering trustworthy sources and citations, guaranteeing that learners and instructors have access to genuine data (D'Souza, 2025). The use of these AI technologies in education also brings up ethical issues, such as openness in AI-generated content, bias reduction, and data protection. Guidelines must be put in place by institutions to guarantee appropriate AI use and optimise its advantages for students (Macinska & Vinkler, 2024). AI will probably play a bigger part in education as it develops further, encouraging creativity and enhancing academic results in a range of subject areas.

Personalised learning, administrative work automation, and adaptive technology that increase student engagement are all examples of how AI is transforming educational practices (Apelehin et al., 2025). AI-powered platforms examine individual learning styles to personalise content, guaranteeing that students receive teaching that is tailored to their needs. Teachers can concentrate more on interactive instruction by using AI to streamline administrative, curriculum creation, and grading processes. New AI technologies that enable collaborative learning settings and offer instant feedback, including generative AI models and intelligent tutoring systems, promote deeper understanding. Ethical issues, like as algorithmic prejudice and data privacy, are still significant problems that need regulatory attention (Al-Kadi & Ali, 2024). The use of AI into education holds potential for more effective and fair educational opportunities as the technology develops.

Researchers examine the effects of AI applications in education, such as ChatGPT, Copilot, DeepSeek, Gemini, Grok, and Perplexity, on learning, the development of cognitive skills, and individualised tutoring. Comparative studies on the efficacy and integration of these tools are warranted due to their distinct strengths, which range from multimodal AI features to research synthesis and conversational engagement. One important area of study is the strategic adoption of several models of AI, which looks at how students use various AI interfaces to maximise learning results. To ensure responsible AI use in education, it is also necessary to look into ethical issues including transparency, algorithmic bias, and data privacy. In order to shape future AI-driven educational frameworks, by examining these aspects, scholars aid in the development of innovative pedagogy and policies.

The current landscape of AI in education

Maximising the potential of AI tools in language education to improve accessibility, engagement, and learning results requires an understanding of the various tools. With features ranging from automated content creation and multimodal interactions to real-time language support and adaptive learning, AI-powered systems like ChatGPT, DeepSeek, Gemini, Grok, and Copilot provide unique capabilities. DeepSeek promotes research-driven analysis, ChatGPT excels in conversational AI, and Gemini makes interactive, multi-format learning experiences easier. Each tool has a distinct purpose. To successfully incorporate these technologies, educators and researchers must evaluate them critically, making sure that they are in line with instructional objectives and taking ethical issues like prejudice and data privacy into account (Tawafak et al., 2023; Tawafak et al., 2025).

As AI develops further, educators may design dynamic, inclusive, and customised learning environments that meet the needs of a wide range of learners by having a sophisticated grasp of these tools. The main AI tools that used in language teaching and learning contexts are:

ChatGPT

ChatGPT is an AI language model that can produce text that looks human, respond to inquiries, and help with a variety of tasks through natural dialogue. Deep learning is used to comprehend context and deliver logical, educational, and imaginative answers. It is a game-changing solution for interactive learning that enhances tailored learning and student engagement through conversational AI (Klimova et al., 2024). Because ChatGPT is an advanced language model, it enables dynamic interactions that let students get immediate feedback, understand concepts, and have meaningful conversations (Barrot, 2023). Its capacity to comprehend spoken language allows students to engage in discourse about difficult subjects, encouraging greater understanding and critical thinking. By offering personalised responses based on each learner's unique needs, AI-driven conversational agents increase accessibility and make education more inclusive and flexible, according to research (Bettayeb et al., 2024; Klimova et al., 2023). The ability of ChatGPT to provide individualised teaching is one of its main educational benefits. According to studies, chatbots driven by AI may mimic one-on-one instruction while adjusting to the learning preferences and skill levels of each learner. This feature is very helpful while learning a language because practicing conversations in real time improves understanding and fluency (Klayklung et al., 2023). Furthermore, ChatGPT helps teachers by automating administrative duties like content creation and grading, freeing them up to concentrate on interactive teaching strategies (Ali et al., 2024;

Hossain & Al Younus, 2025). However, there are also important ethical issues that need to be carefully regulated, such as data privacy and prejudice in AI-generated solutions. Numerous studies have examined the incorporation of ChatGPT into educational frameworks, with research highlighting the technology's potential to completely transform conventional learning settings (Mahapatra, 2024). In order to optimise learning results, it is crucial to strike a balance between pedagogical principles and technical improvements in online courses, according to a comprehensive study of AI uses in education (Al-Obaydi, Shakkib & Pikhart, 2025). As AI develops further, ChatGPT's contribution to interactive learning is anticipated to grow, providing creative answers for individualised instruction while resolving moral dilemmas to guarantee responsible application.

Finally, because ChatGPT provides dynamic, real-time engagement that improves student understanding and fluency, it has become a useful tool in language instruction. With the help of its conversational AI capabilities, language learners can investigate the use of language in context in meaningful ways, practice language skills dynamically, and get immediate feedback. Furthermore, ChatGPT helps teachers by promoting individualised learning experiences, creating activities, and automating content development. Accessibility and engagement are enhanced by its versatility, but responsible and successful incorporation into language instruction requires careful management of ethical issues including the privacy and AI-generated biases.

Copilot

Microsoft's Copilot is an AI companion that supports users' writing, thinking, learning, and creating across platforms and devices. Together with strong features like voice interaction, image production, and real-time reasoning, it integrates conversational intelligence to assist with both simple and intricate tasks (Al-Kadi & Ali, 2024). Copilot is revolutionising education by making structured task management and content creation easier, allowing teachers to improve student engagement and streamline their workflow (Panini, 2024). Copilot is a natural fit for educational settings as an AI-powered assistant that helps with lesson preparation, automated grading, and the production of customised content (Paoli, 2024). With the use of AI-driven insights, users can create adaptable learning programmes that are suited to the needs of each individual student, promoting a more effective and inclusive educational system (Williams, 2024). Research shows that Copilot and other AI-assisted solutions greatly lessen administrative workloads, freeing up teachers to concentrate on engaging and student-centred learning (Al-Kadi & Ali, 2024).

The capacity of Copilot to produce structured educational materials, such as lesson plans, exams, and instructional manuals, is one of its main features

(Williams, 2024). AI-driven automation reduces repetitive work and optimises resource allocation while guaranteeing consistency and accuracy in content creation (HelloCappuccino, 2024). According to Esfandiari & Allaf-Akbary (2024), AI-powered assistants increase productivity by giving teachers data-driven insights and real-time suggestions, which eventually improves learning outcomes. Furthermore, by enabling smooth communication between teachers and students and guaranteeing that educational resources are interesting and easily available, Copilot promotes collaborative learning environments (Pan, 2024).

Ethical issues like data privacy and AI transparency are also brought up by the use of Copilot in the classroom. Establishing policies is necessary to guarantee responsible AI use and optimise its advantages for students (Groves et al., 2024). As AI develops further, Copilot's function in organised work administration and content creation is anticipated to grow, providing creative answers for individualised instruction while resolving moral dilemmas to guarantee responsible application (Barrot, 2023).

As a conclusion, Copilot simplifies the creation of content, offers organised support, and improves individualised learning opportunities, all of which contribute to language instruction. More effective and interesting instruction is made possible by its capacity to assist teachers with lesson planning, automatic feedback, and interactive exercises. Copilot creates adaptable learning environments by incorporating AI-driven insights, allowing students to receive personalised instruction based on their unique development. Although there is no denying that technology can reduce burden and improve accessibility, ethical issues like data privacy and AI bias need to be properly controlled to enable responsible and successful adoption in language instruction.

DeepSeek

DeepSeek is a Chinese AI startup renowned for creating sophisticated large language models and inventing effective training methods. Compatibility with locally made AI chips, tool integration, and organised reasoning are the main features of its most recent model, DeepSeek-V3.1. DeepSeek is a platform driven by generative AI that is meant to improve advanced reasoning and exploration. What makes it unique is that it can give responses that are detailed and relevant to the situation while still using minimal computing power. Traditional AI models focus on giving straight answers, but DeepSeek uses multi-step reasoning chains that let users see how it thinks and play with difficult problem-solving situations (Majeed et al., 2025). Because of this reasoning transparency, DeepSeek is a useful tool for research, education, and decision-making since it promotes greater comprehension and confidence in AI-generated insights.

One of DeepSeek's primary contributions is its methodical way of reasoning, which helps it to efficiently handle lengthy or unclear contexts. The capacity of DeepSeek-R1 to generate intricate reasoning pathways is demonstrated by studies, guaranteeing that answers are not only correct but also logically sound (Turow, 2025). By iterating through several layers of inference before drawing conclusions, DeepSeek replicates human-like analytical processes, according to research on its effects on cognitive modelling. Nevertheless, results also show that too much inference time can occasionally affect performance, indicating that the ideal reasoning length is essential for preserving effectiveness (Marjanović et al., 2025).

DeepSeek's method of reasoning and exploration is having an impact on the creation of other large language models in the larger AI field. Its focus on open-source cooperation and algorithmic efficiency has raised the bar for AI's flexibility and transparency. DeepSeek's techniques provide encouraging avenues for improving structured information retrieval, intelligent search experiences, and the creation of authoritative content as AI develops further (Ali & Khan, 2025). The continuous investigation into its reasoning abilities emphasises how crucial it is to strike a balance between computational effectiveness and in-depth analysis in order to optimise AI's potential across a range of fields (Marjanović et al., 2025).

In conclusion, DeepSeek is an exceptional AI tool for sophisticated thinking and exploration, especially in the fields of research and education. Its capacity to produce organised, multi-step reasoning processes deepens analysis and enables users to interact with scenarios involving intricate problem-solving. Through enhancing algorithmic effectiveness and transparency in AI-generated insights, DeepSeek helps produce more dependable and understandable results. A major obstacle still exists, nevertheless, in striking a balance between depth and processing efficiency. DeepSeek's approaches present exciting avenues for improving academic research, structured information retrieval, and intelligent search experiences as AI develops, making it a useful tool in knowledge-driven industries.

Gemini

Gemini is a powerful multimodal AI model that may be applied to research and teaching because of its capacity to process and generate text, image, and video content. For better understanding and engagement, Gemini incorporates several data formats, in contrast to conventional AI models that only concentrate on text-based interactions (Google Cloud, 2024). Enhancing accessibility and retention, this feature enables students to engage with instructional materials in a variety of ways. Gemini's capabilities to analyse diagrams, understand photos, and create educational movies, for example, can help students studying difficult scientific subjects have a more engaging educational experience (Google DeepMind, 2024).

Gemini's capacity to facilitate multimodal learning settings is one of its main advantages. By presenting information through a variety of sensory channels, multimodal AI models enhance cognitive processing and help learners better understand abstract concepts, according to research (Williams & Roberts, 2024). Gemini's capacity to provide structured responses from text, image, and video inputs makes it especially helpful in fields where comprehension of graphical data is essential, such engineering, medicine, and the visual arts. Furthermore, teachers can design interactive classes that adjust to students' preferred methods of learning thanks to its interaction with cloud-based systems, guaranteeing individualised training (Google DeepMind, 2024).

Notwithstanding its benefits, the use of Gemini in the classroom also brings up moral questions about data privacy and prejudices brought on by AI (Google Cloud, 2024). To guarantee safe AI use and optimise its advantages for students, educational institutions must set rules. Gemini's multimodal capabilities are anticipated to grow as AI advances, providing creative answers for individualised instruction and information sharing (Williams & Roberts, 2024).

In summary, Gemini is a game-changing educational tool because of its multimodal features, which allow students to interact more fully and interactively with text, images, and videos. Gemini boosts retention, speeds up cognitive processing, and creates individualised learning experiences in a variety of fields by combining different data forms. It increases educational opportunities by analysing both verbal and visual content, especially in subjects that call for intricate graphical interpretation. However, to guarantee responsible adoption, ethical issues like data privacy and AI bias need to be properly managed. Gemini is anticipated to play a bigger part in education as AI develops further, providing creative answers for immersive and flexible learning.

Grok

Elon Musk's xAI created the Grok AI model, which is intended for complicated task integration, live search, and real-time reasoning. Grok 4, its most recent version, is perfect for advanced workflows, creativity, and multidisciplinary research because it has PhD-level intelligence and multi-agent collaboration. Grok uses cutting-edge AI capabilities to rapidly handle complicated data in order to provide analysis and insights in real time for dynamic environments. In contrast to conventional models that depend on static datasets, Grok incorporates real-time information streams, allowing users to make defensible choices in light of changing circumstances (Wangsa et al., 2024). In domains where quick data interpretation is essential, such adaptability makes it particularly helpful for tasks like market analysis, crisis management, and financial forecasting. According to studies, Grok's capacity to combine data from several sources improves prediction accuracy, enabling users to foresee patterns and take proactive measures in response (Marjanović et al., 2025).

Grok's sophisticated analytical framework, which allows it to process massive amounts of unstructured data while preserving contextual relevance, is one of its main advantages (Majeed et al., 2025). AI-driven real-time analysis has been shown to enhance decision-making by lowering cognitive burden and yielding useful insights. Grok is a dependable instrument for experts who need up-to-date information because of its connection with dynamic databases, which guarantees that its responses stay current. Its capacity to spot trends and connections in intricate datasets also improves risk assessment and strategic planning (Lei, 2025).

Notwithstanding its benefits, using Grok in dynamic situations has drawbacks, such as issues with data integrity and morality (Wangsa et al., 2024). Maintaining accuracy and confidence in decision-making processes depends on making sure AI-generated insights are transparent. Grok is anticipated to play a bigger part in real-time analysis as AI develops further, providing creative solutions for sectors that depend on quick data interpretation (Lei, 2025). Its prediction powers will probably be optimised in future studies as bias and data integrity issues are addressed.

In conclusion, Grok is a useful tool for dynamic scenarios needing quick data processing and decision-making because of its real-time insight and analysis capabilities. Grok improves prediction accuracy and adaptability by incorporating real-time information streams, which supports applications in areas like strategic planning, crisis management, and financial forecasting. Users can foresee patterns and take preventive measures thanks to its capacity to synthesise complex datasets. To enable responsible adoption, however, issues like data dependability and ethical considerations need to be resolved. Grok's role in real-time analysis is anticipated to grow as AI develops further, providing creative solutions for sectors that depend on real-time insights (Majeed et al., 2025).

Perplexity

Perplexity is an AI-powered search engine that provides accurate and concise knowledge retrieval through state-of-the-art machine learning and natural language processing (NLP) techniques. Perplexity provides direct answers along with citations to credible sources, which improves the efficiency and usability of information retrieval in contrast to standard search engines that return a list of links (Perplexity AI, 2025). By using retrieval-augmented generation (RAG), Perplexity makes sure that answers are supported by reliable references and are contextually relevant, which increases the accuracy and trustworthiness of AI-generated insights (Perplexity AI, 2025).

Analysing user intent and providing accurate results catered to specific searches is one of Perplexity's primary advantages (Smith, & Lee, 2025). Research shows that by lowering cognitive load and doing away with the need for users to navigate across numerous web pages, AI-driven search engines enhance information retrieval. Through time and human interactions, Perplexity's adaptive learning process improves the accuracy of its responses (Johnson & Wang, 2024). Its real-time data retrieval feature also guarantees that users get the most recent information, which makes it an invaluable tool for professional queries, academic study, and general knowledge exploration.

The use of AI-powered search engines, such as Perplexity, has benefits, but it also brings up ethical issues, such as source dependability and data privacy (Johnson & Wang, 2024). To preserve confidence in automatic techniques for retrieving knowledge, it is essential to provide transparency in AI-generated responses. As AI develops further, Perplexity's function in information retrieval is anticipated to grow, providing creative solutions for consumers looking for precise and properly referenced responses in a digital environment that is becoming more and more complicated (Smith, & Lee, 2025).

Ultimately, Perplexity can be described as a sophisticated AI-powered tool for precise and succinct knowledge retrieval, utilising retrieval-augmented generation to improve information accuracy. It makes information more accessible and less cognitively taxing for users looking for trustworthy information by giving straightforward responses with references. It is a priceless resource for scholarly research. because of its capacity to modify responses in response to user interactions, guaranteeing relevance. However, to preserve confidence in insights produced by AI, ethical issues like data privacy and source credibility need to be properly handled. It is anticipated that Perplexity's contribution to knowledge retrieval will grow as AI develops further, providing effective answers for precise and properly referenced data.

A comparison of all these AI tools

With cutting-edge solutions for individualised instruction, increased engagement, and effective content creation, artificial intelligence (AI) applications in education are revolutionising how both students and teachers learn. Programs such as ChatGPT, Copilot, DeepSeek, Gemini, Grok, and Perplexity each bring special capabilities to the educational landscape, addressing various facets of learning and teaching. While some AI models offer multimodal resources, organised content creation, and real-time analysis, others concentrate on adaptive learning and interactive tutoring. Teachers can improve language instruction, research methods, and student engagement by strategically integrating these technologies by being aware of their unique functions. A comparative table outlining each AI tool's advantages and uses in education can be seen in Table 6.

Table 6. A comparative summary of the six AI tools

AI Tool	Advantages	Potential Uses in Teaching
ChatGPT	Interactive learning, real-time feedback, and conversational AI	Conversation-based practice, automated content production, and individualised language instruction
Copilot	Task automation, structured content creation, and assistance with adaptive learning	Personalised instruction, automated grading, and lesson preparation
DeepSeek	Multi-step inference, sophisticated reasoning, and research-driven investigation	Improvement of critical thinking, help with organised research, and scenarios for problem-solving
Gemini	AI-generated explanations that are interactive and multimodal (text, graphics, and video)	Interactive multimedia content, cross-disciplinary participation, and visual learning assistance
Grok	Predictive modelling, real-time insight, and dynamic scenario analysis	Simulations of crisis management, quick data interpretation, and educational strategic planning
Perplexity	Accurate and concise information retrieval using references	Support for academic inquiry, research aid, and effective fact-based learning

As mentioned in Table 6, AI applications in education generally and in language education specifically provide a variety of features to meet various teaching and learning requirements. ChatGPT is a useful tool for individualised language training since it allows for interactive learning through real-time feedback. In contrast, Copilot is a master at creating structured content and automating lesson preparation and grading to reduce the effort of teachers. With its emphasis on sophisticated reasoning and research-driven investigation, DeepSeek supports academic studies by promoting critical thinking and problem-solving. Gemini improves learning through the use of multimodal interactions, which let students interact with text, pictures, and videos to gain a deeper comprehension of difficult subjects. Because of its expertise in predictive modelling and real-time insights, Grok is useful in dynamic situations like strategic planning and crisis management. Perplexity, on the other hand, is notable for its capacity to extract succinct, properly referenced information, hence facilitating rigorous academic research and inquiries. When combined, these AI tools create a more flexible, effective, and interesting learning environment that helps teachers and students use technology to achieve better results while addressing moral issues like bias and data privacy.

The dilemma of using AI applications in language teaching environment

There are advantages and disadvantages of integrating AI technologies into language instruction, which puts institutions and teachers in a dilemma (Derakhshan & Ghiasvand, 2024; Kohnke et al., 2023). While ChatGPT, Copilot, Gemini, Grok, and Perplexity are examples of AI-powered applications that improve personalised learning, automate content creation, and offer real-time insights, they also bring up issues with technological constraints, ethical considerations, and pedagogical efficacy (Al-Kadi & Ali, 2024; Majeed et al., 2025).

The pedagogical effects of AI in language instruction are among the main conundrums. Although AI-driven technologies can offer real-time feedback, grammar clarifications, and conversation practice, they might not have the sophisticated comprehension of human teachers. According to research, although AI can aid in language learning, instructors' contributions to encouraging creativity, critical thinking, and cultural sensitivity cannot be entirely replaced (Al-Zubaidi, 2025). Furthermore, AI-generated responses could not always be contextually suitable, which could result in miscommunications.

Privacy and ethical considerations are a major worry as well. Concerns regarding privacy and data security for students are raised by the fact that AI applications rely on enormous volumes of data to produce answers (Klimova et al., 2023). According to studies, in order to guard against misuse and illegal access to personal data, AI-driven language learning systems need to put strong data protection mechanisms in place (Son et al., 2023). The quality of language instruction can also be impacted by biases in AI-generated information, which can provide false language models or promote preconceptions and also may affect students' emotional engagement and goal oriented (Derakhshan, 2025).

Another problem with AI in language instruction is its technological limits (Al-Obaydi, Shakki & Pikhart, 2025; Doncheva, 2020; Tawafak et al., 2024). AI may have trouble understanding nuanced linguistic nuances, colloquial idioms, and cultural variances (Al-Obaydi & Pikhart, 2023), even though it can automate repetitive operations like grading and content creation (Soroya et al., 2023). According to research, human interaction and ongoing updates are frequently necessary for AI-driven language models to maintain relevance and accuracy (Wu, 2025). Additionally, because students may grow too reliant on automated support, dependence on AI tools may hinder their capacity to acquire autonomous problem-solving abilities.

Nevertheless, AI applications are still developing and providing creative approaches to language learning in spite of these problems. To ensure that language learning experiences are meaningful, educators must find a balance between utilising AI to increase efficiency and preserving human-centred teaching methods. The goal of future study should be to maximise AI's educational potential while tackling pedagogical, technological, and ethical issues.

Practical examples of AI applications

These are a few examples of AI tools being used in education. For example, ChatGPT's potential for second language learning specifically, its ability to explain grammar and facilitate participatory learning has been extensively studied. According to research, conversational agents driven by AI improve language acquisition by offering individualised teaching and real-time feedback. A study done by Han (2024) highlights the value of conducting methodical research on ChatGPT's uses in foreign language instruction, emphasising how well it can mimic real-world language use and facilitate formative evaluation. In discussing ChatGPT's function in second language learning, this Foreword highlights the necessity of doing methodical research to assess its efficacy and ramifications. A different study by Çobanoğulları (2024) explores how ChatGPT enhances conversational and writing skills in foreign languages by providing personalised feedback. In this study, the use of ChatGPT in foreign language instruction is examined, with a focus on responsible use and the potential for improving written and conversational fluency.

Copilot helps teachers by automating material creation, grading, and lesson planning. This lessens administrative work and frees up more time for interactive instruction. AI-driven automation, according to studies, improves productivity in learning environments and guarantees uniformity in course contents. Although there aren't many case studies specifically examining Copilot's educational uses, research on AI-powered teaching aids demonstrates how useful it is for automating tedious chores (Al-Kadi & Ali, 2024).

Because of Gemini's multimodal features, teachers may create interactive lesson plans that combine text, graphics, and videos to create engaging language learning experiences. It has been demonstrated that AI-powered multimedia tools increase understanding and engagement, especially in fields that call for visual interpretation. Multimodal AI models have been shown to be useful in improving cognitive processing and memory (Al-Kadi & Ali, 2024; Williams & Roberts, 2024).

Grok is useful for deciphering colloquial idioms and promoting lively discussions in language instruction because of its real-time analytical capabilities (Majeed et al., 2025). Learners can better understand cultural allusions and subtle meanings with the use of AI-driven models that analyse contextual language usage. There aren't many experimental studies on Grok's use in language learning, but studies on AI-powered dialogue systems back up its ability to increase conversational fluency (Wangsa et al., 2024).

Perplexity AI improves knowledge retrieval by offering succinct, properly referenced answers, which makes it a valuable instrument for scholarly research. AI-powered search engines facilitate research procedures and increase information accessibility while lowering cognitive burden. Research focuses on retrieval-augmented generation (RAG) and shows how well it provides contextually relevant and correct information (Smith, & Lee, 2025).

AI-enhanced learning environments have shown great promise in raising academic achievement, student engagement, and individualised learning. Here are a few noteworthy examples of success. According to Verma (2023) study, students who used AI-powered adaptive learning applications had a 62% increase in test results when compared to those who did not. The AI technology improved understanding and retention by offering individualised feedback and training based on each student's unique learning needs (Verma, 2023). This article examines many AI-powered educational projects, emphasising how they affect adaptive learning, student engagement, and institutional effectiveness. A chatbot driven by artificial intelligence was deployed at the University of Murcia in Spain to help students with questions concerning the campus and academic offerings. In the same article and with 91% accuracy, the chatbot responded to over 38,708 queries, greatly increasing student motivation and information accessibility.

Several countries have effectively incorporated AI into their educational systems, including the US, China, Finland, and India. AI-driven platforms have improved teaching methods and student engagement in Finland, while China has used AI for extensive educational projects (Teachflow. AI, 2022). Institutions have been able to identify students who are at danger of academic failure and offer them targeted support by using AI-powered predictive analytics systems like Civitas Learning. Retention rates and overall academic performance have increased as a result of these approaches (VanWinkle, 2024). These success stories demonstrate AI's transformative power in education by showing how it may improve student results, expedite administrative tasks, and customise learning.

Future vision

AI in education is predicted to revolutionise the field in the future by improving intelligent tutoring programs, adaptive evaluation, and individualised learning (Baker & Inventado, 2024). Through performance analysis and content customisation, AI-powered platforms will keep improving personalised learning experiences (Bahrami et al., 2023). By offering individualised training based on learning patterns, research indicates that AI-powered adaptive learning models increase student engagement and retention. The constraints of conventional one-size-fits-all teaching strategies will be lessened as a result of this move toward individualised education, which will allow pupils to advance at their own speed (Xu & Garcia, 2024).

Automated assessment and feedback systems that incorporate AI are another significant advancement (Wang & Johnson, 2025). With AI capabilities, grading procedures will be streamlined and assignments and tests will receive immediate feedback. AI-assisted grading improves uniformity and efficiency while freeing up teachers to concentrate on more complex teaching assignments, according to studies (Wang & Johnson, 2025). AI-powered writing helpers will also help students enhance their communication and critical thinking abilities by providing real-time feedback (Zawacki-Richter & Latchem, 2023).

With its multilingual support, speech-to-text capabilities, providing customised learning support for individuals with disabilities, AI is also predicted to completely transform educational accessibility (Bahrami et al., 2023). Voice recognition software and AI-powered translation tools will improve access to instructional materials for students from a variety of linguistic backgrounds (Kelly, 2025). Because of this development, learning settings will be more inclusive and knowledge will be accessible to all (Zawacki-Richter & Latchem, 2023).

The ethical issues surrounding AI in education continue to be a significant obstacle in spite of these encouraging advancements (Luckin, 2023). Careful thought must be given to issues like algorithmic bias, data privacy, and the possible over-reliance on AI-driven education. To enable responsible adoption in educational settings, experts stress the necessity of ethical principles and transparent AI rules. To optimise AI's advantages while reducing its risks, educators and legislators must strike a balance between technological advancement and moral principles as the technology develops(Bahrami et al., 2023).

The future of AI in education is directly tied to both technophobia and digital literacy. The ability of users to interact with AI technologies effectively will determine how well they are incorporated into educational settings as they continue to develop. In order to ensure ethical use and critical thinking in the evaluation of material, digital literacy will be essential in educating educators and students to use AI-powered learning tools (Tiernan et al., 2023). Learners may find it difficult to take use of AI's potential for automated assessment, individualised learning, and research efficiency if they lack the necessary digital abilities (Sparks et al., 2024). In light of AI developments, Tiernan et al. (2023) examines how digital literacy frameworks are changing and highlights the necessity of flexible approaches.

The use of AI, however, is hampered by technophobia, which is the fear or hostility to technology, which may also delay its incorporation into the classroom. The revolutionary potential of AI-driven learning will be constrained if teachers and students are hesitant to employ AI because of misunderstandings or a lack of exposure (Naamati-Schneider & Alt, 2024). Building confidence and guaranteeing broad adoption need addressing technophobia through organised training, awareness initiatives, and supervised AI encounters. Pikhart & Al-Obaydi (2023) looks at the difficulties university foreign language instructors encounter when teaching technology-based courses, emphasising problems like technophobia, insufficient training, low student interest, and digital teaching approaches which are all represent a part of future obstacles. These problems are related to one way or another to the situation of language learning where a technology may be used.

Institutions must give digital literacy programmes top priority and get past obstacles brought on by technophobia if AI is to realise its future promise of inclusive, personalised, and adaptable education. The perception, application, and optimisation of AI for significant educational gains will be influenced by these factors. AI has the potential to improve learning effectiveness, accessibility, and customisation in education overall. AI can be used by educational institutions to create dynamic, learning environments that are focused on students by resolving ethical issues and improving AI-driven approaches.

Conclusion

Language instruction has been profoundly changed by the incorporation of AI tools like ChatGPT, Copilot, DeepSeek, Gemini, Grok, and Perplexity, which provide improved personalisation, adaptive learning, and automated feedback systems. These AI models promote content creation, enable interactive conversations, offer immediate grammar corrections, and increase the accessibility of research in foreign language instruction. More autonomy, efficiency, and interest in language learning are guaranteed when learning experiences can be customised to meet the needs of each individual student. Furthermore, by filling in the gaps in communication and instructional support, multimodal learning platforms and AI-powered writing assistants can create more immersive learning environments.

It is worth mentioning that AI language learning apps like ChatGPT, Copilot, DeepSeek, Gemini, Grok, and Perplexity are primarily dependent on user preferences and satisfaction levels, including those of teachers and pupils. Their adoption and use of these resources influence how AI is incorporated into the classroom and establishes its long-term sustainability in the field of education. Students and teachers alike have different expectations and degrees of comfort using AI-powered language tools. AI programs like Copilot and DeepSeek, which facilitate the generation of comprehensive material and the synthesis of research, may appeal to educators who favour analytical frameworks and structure. Conversely, students might give priority to conversational and interactive AI technologies like ChatGPT and Gemini in order to develop fluency and receive immediate feedback. How effectively these apps fit different teaching and learning styles will determine how well AI adoption goes.

The potential of AI tools to improve instructional efficiency without sacrificing traditional teaching ideals will determine how satisfied teachers are with them. Some educators value AI because it frees them up to concentrate on individualised education by automating monotonous activities like feedback and grading. Others could be dubious because they believe AI-generated answers are shallow and not pedagogically sound. For teachers to successfully incorporate AI into their teaching practices while keeping control over curriculum design, training and AI literacy initiatives are essential. However, how well these technologies improve motivation, engagement, and language proficiency will determine how satisfied students are with AI applications. Students can follow customised learning routes and advance at their own speed with the help of AI-driven tutoring programs, adaptive learning platforms, and automated feedback systems. However, some students could find it difficult to understand the technical intricacies of AI technologies or might feel alienated from human-centred learning methods. Maintaining student satisfaction requires making sure AI enhances active engagement rather than takes the place of human connection.

Concerns about AI bias, accuracy, and openness are ethical issues that also affect user satisfaction and his/her preference toward choosing one of these applications. Scepticism could prevent uptake if educators and students believe AI-generated information is untrustworthy or inconsistent with their learning objectives. Educational institutions must use ethical AI frameworks to ensure that AI-generated replies are fact-based, culturally sensitive, and pedagogically competent in order to foster trust. A balanced approach to AI-powered education will be promoted by establishing rules for safe AI use, which will boost user confidence.

Finally, it should be noted that AI's future success in language instruction will rely on its capacity to adjust to a variety of user requirements while upholding pedagogical integrity. In order to ensure user-friendly design, accessible interfaces, and significant learning outcomes, AI developers must improve these applications in response to user feedback. More sophisticated, efficient AI-powered solutions will result from fostering cooperation between educators, students, and AI specialists. Language instruction can be enhanced through purposeful, moral, and technologically advanced learning opportunities by promoting a balanced approach in which AI enhances rather than replaces conventional teaching techniques. In addition to innovation, the future of AI in language instruction depends on its capabilities being responsibly managed so that it can help, not hinder, the development of linguistic fluency and intercultural understanding.

Pedagogical implications

AI systems such as ChatGPT, Copilot, DeepSeek, Gemini, Grok, and Perplexity have important pedagogical ramifications for language learning, influencing how training is provided, learning is tailored, and teaching approaches change. With adaptive learning, automated evaluation, improved linguistic interaction, and the development of critical thinking, these AI-powered tools aid in language acquisition. However, they also present difficulties with regard to pedagogical authenticity, moral dilemmas, and teacher-student relationships.

The potential of AI to develop adaptive learning environments is one of the main pedagogical changes it has brought about. In order to meet the demands of general learners, traditional language training frequently adheres to a prescribed syllabus. However, in order to deliver individualised information and customised lessons, AI-driven systems examine students' involvement, linguistic mistakes, and proficiency. By modifying difficulty levels, offering personalised grammar exercises, and suggesting context-relevant vocabulary improvements, apps such as ChatGPT and Gemini improve learning and guarantee that students receive unique training.

By enabling automatic grading and real-time feedback, AI apps greatly lessen the strain of teachers without sacrificing the quality of instruction. Students can immediately see their mistakes thanks to Copilot and DeepSeek's ability to offer immediate plagiarism detection, essay evaluations, and syntax repair. In addition to promoting self-directed learning, this speeds up formative evaluation and allows students to edit their work without waiting for human feedback. AI lacks human intuition when it comes to judging creativity, cultural appropriateness, and rhetorical efficacy, therefore questions regarding the breadth of AI evaluations still exist.

For language learners who are not exposed to their target language in the actual world, AI applications offer interactive language practice platforms.

Students can improve their pronunciation, fluency, and contextual awareness by using tools like ChatGPT and Gemini, which imitate conversations. By providing a variety of linguistic settings, Grok and Perplexity go beyond this, helping students improve their grammatical accuracy and cultural competency. Though dependence on AI can diminish human-to-human connection, which is crucial to authentic language learning, the pedagogical benefit is evident students receive constant practice.

AI tools improve critical thinking beyond language support by helping students with academic writing, argument creation, and research synthesis. Students can more easily study texts, synthesise conclusions, and assess sources with the help of DeepSeek and Copilot's organised citation management frameworks. Teachers must make sure that AI is utilised as an additional tool rather than as a substitute for autonomous thought, even while this improves students' analytical skills. Students' capacity to critically assess arguments and cultivate creativity in academic discourse may be hampered by an excessive dependence on AI-generated material.

AI-driven education has pedagogical ramifications that go beyond moral dilemmas and changing teacher roles. Teachers must rethink their teaching strategies in light of AI's ability to automate some aspects of instruction. They should concentrate on contextualisation, interpretation, and direction rather than merely imparting knowledge. Furthermore, it is difficult to guarantee impartial and equitable learning experiences due to AI's possible biases, accuracy issues, and ethical transparency. In order to protect student privacy and encourage responsible AI use, educational institutions must set explicit ethical standards for AI use.

The future of AI in the process of language learning depends on its integration in a way that is both balanced and pedagogically good, where it enhances rather than replaces conventional teaching methods. In order to combine the human-centric elements of critical thinking, interpersonal communication, and cultural immersion with AI's effectiveness in adaptive learning, assessment, and research, educators must embrace hybrid approaches. AI's potential to automate instruction, increase access, and customise education must be carefully managed to maintain pedagogical legitimacy while promoting creative and inclusive language learning opportunities.

Conclusion

The integration of digital technologies into foreign language education has ushered in a transformative era, reshaping pedagogical approaches, learner engagement, and cognitive development. This book has explored the latest trends, theoretical foundations, and ethical considerations surrounding digital tools, AI, and game-based learning in language education. The possibilities for individualised and adaptable learning have increased due to the quick development of digital technologies, which range from immersive virtual environments to AI-driven tutoring systems. The way that language learners engage with language information is being redefined by emerging technologies like chatbots driven by artificial intelligence (AI), virtual reality (VR), and augmented reality (AR).

There might be generational differences. For example, elderly people have particular difficulties, such as hurdles to digital literacy, whereas younger students frequently engage with digital platforms intuitively. However, this disparity can be closed by using user-friendly interfaces and customised instructional designs, guaranteeing equal access to online language learning resources. Digital technologies improve cognitive abilities like language processing, pattern identification, and memory retention. Deeper involvement is encouraged via gamified learning settings and AI-driven feedback systems, which enhance language acquisition and retention over time. A potent instrument for language instruction, game-based learning provides engaging, interactive experiences that boost motivation and contextual awareness.

The book's applicability to language teachers has been enhanced by a more thorough incorporation of language-specific pedagogical issues, such as vocabulary learning, pronunciation assistance, and cross-cultural communication. In addition to reflecting the complex requirements of digital language acquisition, these dimensions also draw attention to the special opportunities presented by new technologies. In order to provide practitioners with a more focused and useful framework for navigating the changing terrain of language teaching, the book places these opportunities within larger digital trends.

Theoretical theories that offer insights for optimising game-based instruction include Cognitive Load Theory and Multimodal Learning Theory. The power of game-based learning to produce engaging, motivating, and contextually relevant learning experiences in foreign language instruction has been well acknowledged. Digital games can improve language skills and promote cognitive engagement by including aspects of storytelling, competitiveness, and problem-solving. Furthermore, the notion that game-based learning maximises comprehension by delivering language in diverse and significant situations is supported by theories like Multimodal Learning Theory and Cognitive Load Theory. The debate makes a clearer distinction between broad educational ideas and their practical applicability to digital language acquisition in order to improve conceptual clarity. Although constructivism, self-determination theory, and UTAUT2 are useful frameworks for understanding learner behaviour and technology adoption, their implications for language-specific processes like affective engagement, communicative interaction, and linguistic scaffolding need careful consideration. Instead of being used in general, uniform ways, this distinction enables a more accurate understanding of how theoretical models affect practical decisions in digitally mediated language instruction.

Language education has seen a dramatic change as a result of the adoption of AI-powered programs like ChatGPT, Copilot, Gemini, and others. Traditional teaching approaches have given way to flexible, data-driven learning settings. Through the use of advanced natural language processing (NLP) models, these technologies offer individualised training, allowing students to get assistance that is specific to their cognitive preferences, learning styles, and competence levels. AI-powered tools continuously improve their teaching strategies based on real-time learner interactions, creating a more dynamic and responsive learning environment than traditional curricula that rely on static content and standardised tests. Additionally, by providing dynamic, multimodal experiences that integrate text, speech, visuals, and gamification components to encourage language acquisition in natural and engaging ways, AI apps improve learner engagement. With automated feedback systems, sophisticated evaluation models, and culturally diversified language resources, artificial intelligence (AI) is becoming more and more of a cognitive partner in language education, going beyond mere tutoring. However, in order to maintain AI-driven learning's accessibility, equity, and pedagogical soundness, this shift calls for thorough evaluation of its ethical ramifications. Educators and researchers may fully utilise AI to develop enriched, inclusive, and future-ready language learning ecosystems by embracing its capabilities while preserving the fundamentally human elements of language instruction.

Ethical issues pertaining to algorithmic prejudice, data privacy, and fair access must be addressed as digital technologies proliferate. To ensure responsible deployment, transparent AI governance, ethical AI design, and inclusive digital policy are crucial. Ethical issues must continue to be at the forefront of educational discourse as digital technologies continue to influence foreign language instruction. Data privacy is one of the most urgent issues because AI-powered systems frequently gather a lot of user data in order to tailor educational experiences. To preserve learner trust and safeguard sensitive data, it is essential to make sure that this data is securely managed. Furthermore, algorithmic bias in AI language tools may inadvertently harm particular linguistic groups by restricting access to various language resources or perpetuating prejudices. Fairness, inclusivity, and transparency in the creation of learning models should be given top priority in ethical AI research. Equitable access to digital technologies for people from different socio-economic origins presents another ethical dilemma. By giving preference to those who have more access to digital devices, high-speed internet, and technological proficiency, sophisticated technologies run the risk of widening the digital divide even though they present previously unheard-of learning opportunities. In order to ensure that everyone has access to digital resources, regardless of financial or geographic limitations, educational officials must endeavour to establish accessible learning environments. Furthermore, the function of human educators is called into question by the growing dependence on AI for instruction. Even though AI can support instructional methods, ethical frameworks must guarantee that critical thinking and human connection are still essential to learning in order to avoid becoming overly dependent on automated systems. Digital language education may promote inclusivity, equity, and ethical integrity by tackling these ethical issues through responsible innovation and proactive policymaking.

While there are important wider educational ramifications to digitalisation, it is crucial to highlight the precise ways in which new technologies like AI tutors, adaptive learning platforms, and digital games are changing language learning methods. By lowering fear and raising motivation, these technologies improve affective engagement, promote communicative competence through immersive, interaction-rich environments, and enable increased learner autonomy through tailored feedback and self-paced advancement. These affordances place digital technologies in the role of dynamic mediators of language development rather than just instructional aids.

This work highlights the need for focused techniques that use AI tutors, adaptive systems, and game-based platforms to foster autonomy, emotional resilience, and communicative fluency by more explicitly describing the pedagogical impact of digital tools within language instruction. A more nuanced and practice-focused conversation that connects general digital innovation with the unique requirements of language acquisition is encouraged by acknowledging these technologies as drivers of language-specific transformation.

Future teaching approaches in foreign language education could be totally revolutionised by AI since it provides personalised, adaptable, and interesting learning experiences. Speech recognition software, intelligent feedback systems, and language tutors driven by AI have already shown that they can improve understanding and engagement. AI will probably be crucial in the future in developing dynamic, context-sensitive learning environments that are suited to the linguistic objectives and cognitive processes of specific learners. By using deep learning models, AI tutors will be able to assess student performance and provide accurate, in-the-moment interventions, closing the gap between fully adaptive learning and traditional instruction. Even while AI-driven education has great promise, the future must be carefully negotiated to steer clear of pedagogical and ethical issues. AI must be used in conjunction with human instructors, not in place of them, to ensure that students acquire critical thinking, creativity, and interpersonal communication skills. Additionally, enhancing AI's use in language learning, avoiding technological determinism, and guaranteeing pedagogical soundness will require interdisciplinary cooperation between linguists, technologists, and educators. Strong regulatory frameworks to protect moral AI practices and guarantee that AI-generated tests, materials, and interactions adhere to pedagogical standards are also essential components of the future of AI in education. AI has the ability to take language instruction to previously unheard-of levels of efficiency and personalisation while preserving its function as a tool for meaningful learning rather than an independent teacher by striking a balance between innovation and human-centred ideals.

Bibliography

Adamopoulou, E., & Moussiades, L. (2020). Chatbots: History, technology, and applications. Machine Learning with Applications, 2, 100006. https://doi.org/10.1016/j.mlwa.2020.100006

Adipat, S., Laksana, K., Busayanon, K., Asawasowan, A., & Adipat, B. (2021). Engaging students in the learning process with game-based learning: The fundamental concepts. International Journal of Technology in Education (IJTE), 4(3), 542–552. https://doi.org/10.46328/ijte.169

Afzal, A., Khan, S., Daud, S., Ahmad, Z., & Butt, A. (2023). Addressing the Digital Divide: Access and Use of Technology in Education. Journal of Social Sciences Review, 3(2), 883–895. https://doi.org/10.54183/jssr.v3i2.326

Ahadzadeh, A. S., Wu, S. L., & Sijia, X. (2024). Exploring academic intentions for ChatGPT: A perspective from the theory of planned behavior. ASR Chiang Mai University Journal of Social Sciences and Humanities, 11(1), e2024016. https://doi.org/10.12982/CMUJASR.2024.016

Ahmad, N. A., Abd Rauf, M. F., Mohd Zaid, N. N., & Rosli, R. S. (2022). Effectiveness of instructional strategies designed for older adults in learning digital technologies: A systematic literature review. SN COMPUT. SCI., 3, 130. https://doi.org/10.1007/s42979-022-01016-0

Alahmari, M., Jdaitawi, M. T., Rasheed, A., Abduljawad, R., Hussein, E., Alzahrani, M., & Awad, N. (2023). Trends and gaps in empirical research on gamification in science education: A systematic review of the literature. Contemporary Educational Technology, 15(3), ep431. https://doi.org/10.30935/cedtech/13177

Alamer, A. (2016). The Role of EFL Learning' motivation in Mobile Language Learning. Asia Pacific Institute of Advanced Research (APIAR), 2(1), 121–132.

Al-Aosail, A. B. F., Lamouchi, A., Ibrahim, S. A., Gafar, M. G., & Hafez, W. E. (2024). Digital games for learning vocabulary: The effects on foreign language anxiety, buoyancy, online engagement, and vocabulary learning. Computer-Assisted Language Learning Electronic Journal.

Al-Huwail, N., Al-Hunaiyyan, A., Alainati, S., & Alhabshi, A. (2025). Artificial intelligence in education: Perspectives and challenges. International Journal of Interactive Mobile Technologies (iJIM), 19(4), 26–47. https://doi.org/10.3991/ijim.v19i04.52117

Ali, D., Fatemi, Y., Boskabadi, E., Nikfar, M., Ugwuoke, J., & Ali, H. (2024). ChatGPT in Teaching and Learning: A Systematic Review. Education Sciences, 14(6), 643. https://doi.org/10.3390/educsci14060643

Ali, J. K. M., Shamsan, M. A. A., Hezam, T. A., & Mohammed, A. A. Q. (2023). Impact of ChatGPT on learning motivation: Teachers and students' voices. Journal of English Studies in Arabia Felix, 2(1), 41–49. https://doi.org/10.56540/jesaf.v2i1.51

Ali, O., Murray, P. A., Momin, M., Dwivedi, Y. K., & Malik, T. (2024). The effects of artificial intelligence applications in educational settings: Challenges and strategies. Technological Forecasting and Social Change, 199, 123076. https://doi.org/10.1016/j.techfore.2023.123076

Ali, Y. A., & Khan, S. I. (2025). Teachers' perspective on integrating DeepSeek in Saudi EFL classrooms. Journal of Applied Linguistics and Technology, 8(1).

Ali, Z. (2020). Artificial Intelligence (AI): A review of its uses in language teaching and learning. IOP Conference Series: Materials Science and Engineering, 769, 012043. https://doi.org/10.1088/1757-899X/769/1/012043

Al-Kadi, A., & Ali, J. K. M. (2024). A holistic approach to ChatGPT, Gemini, and Copilot in English learning and teaching. Language Teaching Research Quarterly, 43, 155–166. https://doi.org/10.32038/ltrq.2024.43.09

Al-Obaydi, L. H., & Pikhart, M. (2022). A qualitative evaluation of the impact of online visually based L2 acquisition on college students' risk-taking, motivation, and anxiety. Language Related Research, 13(5), 281–301. https://doi.org/10.52547/LRR.13.5.10

Al-Obaydi, L. H., & Pikhart, M. (2023). The evaluation of cultural intelligence enhancement through documentary videos for L2 acquisition. MEXTESOL Journal, 47(1), 1–15. https://doi.org/10.61871/mj.v47n1-5

Al-Obaydi, L. H., Pikhart, M., & Klimova, B. (2023). Verifying EFL autonomous learning by digital gaming: Definitions and concepts. International Journal of Emerging Technologies in Learning, 18(05), 253–260. https://doi.org/10.3991/ijet.v18i05.36617

Al-Obaydi, L. H., Pikhart, M., & Shakki, F. (2023). Digital Gaming as a Panacea for Incidental L2 Acquisition in an EFL Context. Applied Research on English Language, 12(1). https://doi.org/10.22108/ARE.2022.135344.2001

Al-Obaydi, L. H., Pikhart, M., & Shakki, F. (2025). How does emergency remote teaching affect EFL students' writing skills? Cogent Education, 12(1), 2500001. https://doi.org/10.1080/2331186X.2025.2500001

Al-Obaydi, L. H., Pikhart, M., Tawafak, R. M., & Klimova, B. (2025). Relationship investigation between time investment and language learning based on digital games. International Journal of Serious Games, 12(1), 39–57. https://doi.org/10.17083/ijsg.v12i1.845

Al-Obaydi, L. H., Rahul, D. R., & Pikhart, M. (2023). The effect of online oral reading on reading comprehension, reading anxiety, and classroom anxiety among EFL learners. Education and Information Technologies. https://doi.org/10.1007/s10639-023-11950-y

Al-Obaydi, L. H., Shakki, F., Tawafak, R. M., Pikhart, M., & Ugla, R. L. (2023). What I know, what I want to know, what I learned: Activating EFL college students' cognitive, behavioral, and emotional engagement through structured feedback in an online environment. Front. Psychol., 13, 1083673. https://doi.org/10.3389/fpsyg.2022.1083673

Al-Obaydi, L. H., Pikhart, M., & Klimova, B. (2023). ChatGPT and the General Concepts of Education: Can Artificial Intelligence-Driven Chatbots Support the Process of Language Learning? International Journal of Emerging Technologies in Learning (iJET), 18(21), 39–50. https://doi.org/10.3991/ijet.v18i21.42593

Alrayes, A., Henari, T. F., & Ahmed, D. A. (2024). ChatGPT in education – Understanding the Bahraini academics perspective. The Electronic Journal of e-Learning, 22(2), 112–134. https://doi.org/10.34190/ejel.22.2.3250

Alyaz, Y., & Genc, Z. S. (2016). Digital game-based language learning in foreign language teacher education. Turkish Online Journal of Distance Education, 17(4), Article 9. https://dergipark.org.tr/en/pub/tojde/issue/24967/263484

Al-Zubaidi, K. (2025). The challenges of artificial intelligence in English language teaching, learning, and academic publications: Foreword. Arab World English Journal (AWEJ) Special Issue on Artificial Intelligence, 12(1), 1–2. https://ssrn.com/abstract=5239852

Al-Zubaidi, K., Jaafari, M., & Touzani, F. Z. (2024). Impact of ChatGPT on academic writing at Moroccan universities. Arab World English Journal (AWEJ) Special Issue on ChatGPT, April 2024, 4–25.

Ansari, J. A. N., & Khan, N. A. (2020). Exploring the role of social media in collaborative learning the new domain of learning. Smart Learn. Environ., 7, 9. https://doi.org/10.1186/s40561-020-00118-7

Apelehin, A. A., Imohiosen, C. E., Ajuluchukwu, P., Abutu, D. E., Udeh, C. A., Okonkwo, C. A., Iguma, D. R., & Bristol-Alagbariya, B. (2025). Reviewing the role of artificial intelligence in personalized learning and education. World Journal of Innovation and Modern Technology, 9(2), 86–94. https://doi.org/10.56201/wjimt.v9.no2.2025.pg86.94

Aprea, C., & Ifenthaler, D. (2021). Looking Back and Moving Forward with Game-Based Learning Across the Disciplines. In C. Aprea & D. Ifenthaler (Eds.), Game-based Learning Across the Disciplines.

Advances in Game-Based Learning. Springer, Cham. https://doi.org/10.1007/978-3-030-75142-5_18

Arora, L., Choudhary, A., Bhatt, M., Kaliappan, J., & Srinivasan, K. (2024). A comprehensive review on NUI, multi-sensory interfaces and UX design for applications and devices for visually impaired users. Frontiers in Public Health, 12, Article 1357160. https://doi.org/10.3389/fpubh.2024.1357160

Avidov-Ungar, O., & Hayak, M. (2023). Education and Games: Teachers' Professional Knowledge in Integrating Digital Games into Instruction in School. IntechOpen. https://doi.org/10.5772/intechopen.109594

Bader, M., Cloarec, M., Goumy, M., & Hussein, D. (2022). The advantages and limits of gamification mechanisms: A Duolingo case study. Paris Cité University.

Bagherpour, N., Hajirostam, S., & Farjami, A. (2022). The impact of digital games on students' willingness to communicate in a flipped classroom context. Journal of Contemporary Language Research, 1(2), 96–104. http://jclr.rovedar.com/

Bahrami, M. R., Bahrami, B., Behboodi, F., & Pourrafie, S. (2023). Teaching the Future: The Vision of AI/ChatGPT in Education. In G. Jezic, J. Chen-Burger, M. Kusek, R. Sperka, R. J. Howlett, & L. C. Jain (Eds.), Agents and Multi-agent Systems: Technologies and Applications 2023. KES-AMSTA 2023. Smart Innovation, Systems and Technologies, 354. Springer, Singapore. https://doi.org/10.1007/978-981-99-3068-5_37

Bailey, F., & Fahad, A. K. (2021). Krashen revisited: Case study of the role of input, motivation, and identity in second language learning. Arab World English Journal, 12(2), 540–550. https://dx.doi.org/10.24093/awej/vol12no2.36

Baker, R. S., & Inventado, P. S. (2024). Adaptive learning systems and personalized education: AI-driven insights. Computers & Education, 184, 104563. https://doi.org/10.1016/j.compedu.2024.104563

Bancha, W., & Tongtep, N. (2021). Enhancing vocabulary memorization and retention through LMS and MultiEx game platforms among Thai tertiary students. International Journal of Learning, Teaching and Educational Research, 20(10), 173–192.

Barrot, J. S. (2023). ChatGPT as a Language Learning Tool: An Emerging Technology Report. Technology, Knowledge and Learning. https://doi.org/10.1007/s10758-023-09711-4

Bećirović, S., Brdarević-Čeljo, A., & Delić, H. (2021). The use of digital technology in foreign language learning. SN Social Sciences, 1(10), 246. https://doi.org/10.1007/s43545-021-00254-y

Bettayeb, A. M., Abu Talib, M., Sobhe Altayasinah, A. Z., & Dakalbab, F. (2024). Exploring the impact of ChatGPT: conversational AI in education. Front. Educ., 9, 1379796. https://doi.org/10.3389/feduc.2024.1379796

Bin-Hady, W. R. A., Ali, J. K. M., & Al-humari, M. A. (2024). The effect of ChatGPT on EFL students' social and emotional learning. Journal of Research in Innovative Teaching & Learning, 17(2), 243–255. https://doi.org/10.1108/JRIT-02-2024-0036

Bouzar, A., El Idrissi, K., & Ghourdou, T. (2024). Gender differences in perceptions and usage of ChatGPT. International Journal of Humanities and Educational Research, 6(2), 571–582.

Burmich, A., Mashkin, O., & Stepanova, N. (2023). The Role of Game-Based Assessment for the Enhancement of Learning. In D. Bylieva & A. Nordmann (Eds.), The World of Games: Technologies for Experimenting, Thinking, Learning. PCSF 2023. Lecture Notes in Networks and Systems, 830. Springer, Cham. https://doi.org/10.1007/978-3-031-48020-1_27

Cambridge English. (n.d.). Types of activities and tasks for language and skills development. Retrieved from https://www.cliffsnotes.com/study-notes/4562256

Campos, D. G., & Scherer, R. (2024). Digital gender gaps in students' knowledge, attitudes and skills: An integrative data analysis across 32 countries. Education and Information Technologies, 29, 655–693. https://doi.org/10.1007/s10639-023-12272-9

Cao, J., Bhuvaneswari, G., Arumugam, T., & Aravind, B. R. (2023). The digital edge: examining the relationship between digital competency and language learning outcomes. Front. Psychol., 14, 1187909. https://doi.org/10.3389/fpsyg.2023.1187909

CEFR. (2020). Common European Framework of Reference for Languages: Learning, teaching, assessment. Council of Europe. https://rm.coe.int/common-european-framework-of-reference-for-languages-learning-teaching/16809ea0d4

Cerezo-Pizarro, M., Revuelta-Domínguez, F.-I., Guerra-Antequera, J., & Melo-Sánchez, J. (2023). The Cultural Impact of Video Games: A Systematic Review of the Literature. Education Sciences, 13(11), 1116. https://doi.org/10.3390/educsci13111116

Chan, S., & Lo, N. (2024). Enhancing EFL/ESL instruction through gamification: A comprehensive review of empirical evidence. Frontiers in Education, 9. https://doi.org/10.3389/feduc.2024.1395155

Chardonnens, S. (2025). Adapting educational practices for Generation Z: Integrating metacognitive strategies and artificial intelligence. Frontiers in Education, 10, 1504726. https://doi.org/10.3389/feduc.2025.1504726

Chen, C.-C., & Tu, H.-Y. (2021). The Effect of Digital Game-Based Learning on Learning Motivation and Performance Under Social Cognitive Theory and Entrepreneurial Thinking. Front. Psychol., 12, 750711. https://doi.org/10.3389/fpsyg.2021.750711

Chen, C., Ding, S., & Wang, J. (2023). Digital health for aging populations. Nature Medicine, 29, 1623–1630. https://doi.org/10.1038/s41591-023-02391-8

Chiu, L. L., & Liu, G. Z. (2013). Effects of printed, pocket electronic, and online dictionaries on high school students' English vocabulary retention. Asia-Pacific Edu Res, 22, 619–634. https://doi.org/10.1007/s40299-013-0065-1

Chu, C. H., Nyrup, R., Leslie, K., Shi, J., Bianchi, A., Lyn, A., McNicholl, M., Khan, S., Rahimi, S., & Grenier, A. (2022). Digital ageism: Challenges and opportunities in artificial intelligence for older adults. The Gerontologist, 62(7), 947–955. https://doi.org/10.1093/geront/gnab167

Çiftçi, S. (2018). The studies on educational digital games regarding children: A new word analysis approach. TOJET, The Turkish Online Journal of Educational Technology, 17(2), 160–170.

Çobanoğulları, F. (2024). Learning and teaching with ChatGPT: Potentials and applications in foreign language education. The EuroCALL Review, 31(1), 4–15. https://doi.org/10.4995/EUROCALL.2024.19957

Cornillie, F., Clarebout, G., & Desmet, P. (2012). The role of feedback in foreign language learning through digital role-playing games. Procedia - Social and Behavioral Sciences, 34, 49–53.

Cui, C. (2016). A Study of Digital Games as a New Media of Cultural Transmission. In Z. Pan, A. Cheok, W. Müller, & M. Zhang (Eds.), Transactions on Edutainment XII. Lecture Notes in Computer Science, 9292. Springer, Berlin, Heidelberg. https://doi.org/10.1007/978-3-662-50544-1_4

Darin, T., Carneiro, N., Miranda, D., & Coelho, B. (2023). Challenges in Evaluating Players' Interaction with Digital Games. In R. P. D. Santos & M. D. S. Hounsell (Eds.), Grand Research Challenges in Games and Entertainment Computing in Brazil - GranDGamesBR 2020–2030. Communications in Computer and Information Science, 1702. Springer, Cham. https://doi.org/10.1007/978-3-031-27639-2_1

de Freitas, S. (2018). Are games effective learning tools? A review of educational games. Educational Technology & Society, 21(2), 74–84.

Dehghanzadeh, H. (2021). Effects of digital games on critical thinking: Empirical evidence-based study. Paper presented at the 6th International Conference on Computer Games: Challenges and Opportunities, University of Isfahan, Isfahan, Iran.

Derakhshan, A. (2021). Emergence Distance Education (EDE) role in the Learning of English Language Skills during COVID-19 Pandemic. Journal of Teaching Language Skills, 40(3), 41–82. https://doi.org/10.22099/jtls.2021.39849.2948

Derakhshan, A. (2025). EFL students' perceptions about the role of generative artificial intelligence (GAI)-mediated instruction in their emotional engagement and goal orientation: A motivational climate theory (MCT) perspective in focus. Learning and Motivation, 90(1). https://doi.org/10.1016/j.lmot.2025.102114

Derakhshan, A., & Ghiasvand, F. (2024). Is ChatGPT an evil or an angel for second language education and research? A phenomenographic study of research-active EFL teachers' perceptions. International Journal of Applied Linguistics, 1–19. https://doi.org/10.1111/ijal.12561

Derakhshan, A., Eslami, Z. R., & Shakki, F. (2023). Comparing compliments in Face-to-Face vs. online interactions among Iranian speakers of Persian. Pragmatics and Society. https://doi.org/10.1075/ps.22102.der.

Di Giacomo, D., Ranieri, J., & Lacasa, P. (2017). Digital learning as enhanced learning processing? Cognitive evidence for new insight of smart learning. Frontiers in Psychology, 8, 1329. https://doi.org/10.3389/fpsyg.2017.01329

Dizon, G. (2016). Quizlet in the EFL classroom: Enhancing vocabulary acquisition of Japanese university students. Teaching English with Technology, 16(2), 40–56. http://www.tewtjournal.org

Doncheva, J. (2020). Digital technologies in support of the educational process in the world around us, Man and society, Man and nature. Angel Kanchev University Publishing Center, PRIMAX, Primax, 2020, pp. 317.

D'Souza, R. (2025). AI in academia: Comparing ChatGPT, DeepSeek, Perplexity, and Gemini. Enago Academy. Retrieved from Enago.

Du, J., & Alm, A. (2024). The impact of ChatGPT on English for Academic Purposes (EAP) students' language learning experience: A self-determination theory perspective. Education Sciences, 14, 726.

Duong, C., Vu, T., & Ngo, T. (2023). Applying a modified technology acceptance model to explain higher education students' usage of ChatGPT. International Journal of Management Education, 21(3), 100883.

Esfandiari, R., & Allaf-Akbary, O. (2024). Assessing interactional metadiscourse in EFL writing through intelligent data-driven learning: the Microsoft Copilot in the spotlight. Lang Test Asia, 14, 51. https://doi.org/10.1186/s40468-024-00326-9

Essafi, M., Belfakir, L., & Moubtassime, M. (2024). Investigating mobile-assisted language learning apps: Babbel, Memrise, and Duolingo as a case study. Journal of Curriculum and Teaching, 13(2), 197–213. https://doi.org/10.5430/jct.v13n2p197

Essien, A., Bukoye, O. T., O'Dea, X., & Kremantzis, M. (2024). The influence of AI text generators on critical thinking skills in UK business schools. Studies in Higher Education, 49(5), 865–882.

EU. (2020). Digital education action plan (2021–2027): Resetting education and training for the digital age. Publications Office of the European Union. https://education.ec.europa.eu/sites/default/files/document-library-docs/deap-communication-sept2020_en.pdf

Fang, Z., Liu, Y., & Peng, B. (2024). Empowering older adults: bridging the digital divide in online health information seeking. Humanit Soc Sci Commun, 11, 1748. https://doi.org/10.1057/s41599-024-04312-7

Farrokhnia, M., Banihashem, S. K., Noroozi, O., & Wals, A. (2024). A SWOT analysis of ChatGPT: Implications for educational practice and research. Innovations in Education and Teaching International, 61(3), 460–474. https://doi.org/10.1080/14703297.2023.2195846

Faverio, M. (2022). Share of those 65 and older who are tech users has grown in the past decade. Pew Research Center. https://www.pewresearch.org/fact-tank/2022/01/13/share-of-those-65-and-older-who-are-tech-users-has-grown-in-the-past-decade/

Febrianti, M., Rahmawati, I. N., Aisyah, A., Nasution, A. K. P., & Aprianto, A. (2024). Using the Duolingo application as a vocabulary learning tool in higher education. Journal International of Lingua and Technology, 3(2), 345–361. https://doi.org/10.55849/jiltech.v3i2.673

Feretzakis, G., & Verykios, V. S. (2024). Trustworthy AI: Securing sensitive data in large language models. AI, 5(4), 2773–2800.

Fong, B. Y. F., Yee, H. H. L., & Ng, T. K. C. (2022). The use of technology for online learning among older adults in Hong Kong. International Review of Education, 68, 389–407. https://doi.org/10.1007/s11159-022-09957-7

Fulya Eyupoglu, T., & Nietfeld, J. L. (2019). Intrinsic Motivation in Game-Based Learning Environments. In D. Ifenthaler & Y. J. Kim (Eds.), Game-Based Assessment Revisited. Advances in Game-Based Learning. Springer, Cham. https://doi.org/10.1007/978-3-030-15569-8_5

Gee, E., & Gao, Y. (2022). Digital game-mediated language learning for adults. Adult Literacy Education, 4(1), 67–73. https://doi.org/10.35847/EGee.YGao.4.1.67

Gee, J. P. (2003). What video games have to teach us about learning and literacy. Palgrave Macmillan.

George Pallivathukal, R., Kyaw Soe, H. H., Donald, P. M., Samson, R. S., & Hj Ismail, A. R. (2024). ChatGPT for academic purposes: Survey among undergraduate healthcare students in Malaysia. Cureus, 16(1), e53032. https://doi.org/10.7759/cureus.53032

Ghafar, Z. N., Salh, H. F., Abdulrahim, M. A., Farxha, S. S., Arf, S. F., & Rahim, R. I. (2023). The role of artificial intelligence technology on English language learning: A literature review. Canadian Journal of Language and Literature Studies, 3(2), 17–31.

Gherheş, V., Stoian, C. E., Fărcaşiu, M. A., & Stanici, M. (2021). E-learning vs. face-to-face learning: Analyzing students' preferences and behaviors. Sustainability, 13(8), 4381.

Gligorea, I., Cioca, M., Oancea, R., Gorski, A.-T., Gorski, H., & Tudorache, P. (2023). Adaptive learning using Artificial Intelligence in e-Learning: A literature review. Education Sciences, 13(12), 1216. https://doi.org/10.3390/educsci13121216

Godsk, M., & Møller, K. L. (2025). Engaging students in higher education with educational technology. Educ Inf Technol, 30, 2941–2976. https://doi.org/10.1007/s10639-024-12901-x

Gomathi, A. (2024). Faculty perspectives on the adoption of AI tools in education and research. Humanities and Social Science Studies, 13(2), 66–72.

Gómez-Soria, I., Iguacel, I., Aguilar-Latorre, A., Peralta-Marrupe, P., Latorre, E., Cuenca Zaldívar, J. N., & Calatayud, E. (2023). Cognitive stimulation and cognitive results in older adults: A systematic review and meta-analysis. Archives of Gerontology and Geriatrics, 104, 104807. https://doi.org/10.1016/j.archger.2022.104807

Google Cloud. (2024). Gemini 2.0 (experimental) | Generative AI on Vertex AI - Google Cloud. Retrieved from https://cloud.google.com/vertex-ai/generative-ai/docs/gemini-v2

Google DeepMind. (2024). Gemini - Google DeepMind. Retrieved from https://deepmind.google/technologies/gemini/

Granic, I., Lobel, A., & Engels, R. C. (2014). The benefits of playing video games. American Psychologist, 69(1), 66–78. https://doi.org/10.1037/a0034857

Gros, B. (2007). Digital games in education: The design of games-based learning environments. Journal of Research on Technology in Education, 40(1), 23–38. https://files.eric.ed.gov/fulltext/EJ826060.pdf

Gros, B. (2015). Integration of Digital Games in Learning and E-learning Environments: Connecting Experiences and Context. In T. Lowrie & R. Jorgensen (Zevenbergen) (Eds.), Digital Games and Mathematics Learning. Mathematics Education in the Digital Era, 4. Springer, Dordrecht. https://doi.org/10.1007/978-94-017-9517-3_3

Grossmann, J. A., Aschenbrenner, S., Teichmann, B., & Meyer, P. (2023). Foreign language learning can improve response inhibition in individuals with lower baseline cognition. Frontiers in Aging Neuroscience, 15, 1123185. https://doi.org/10.3389/fnagi.2023.1123185

Groves, M., Garralda Ortega, Á., Ting, A., & Zou, D. (2024). Using Microsoft Copilot to Paraphrase in Eap: An Exploratory Study of its Potentials and Pitfalls. http://dx.doi.org/10.2139/ssrn.4962522

Gu, J. (2024). Digital tools in language learning: Optimizing memory and attention for college students. International Journal of Human–Computer Interaction, 1–11. https://doi.org/10.1080/10447318.2024.2400384

Gui, Y., Cai, Z., Yang, Y., & Li, M. (2023). Effectiveness of digital educational game and game design in STEM learning: a meta-analytic review. IJ STEM Ed, 10, 36. https://doi.org/10.1186/s40594-023-00424-9

Gundersen, S. W., & Lampropoulos, G. (2025). Using Serious Games and Digital Games to Improve Students' Computational Thinking and Programming Skills in K-12 Education: A Systematic Literature Review. Technologies, 13(3), 113. https://doi.org/10.3390/technologies13030113

Haase, K. R., Cosco, T., Kervin, L., Riadi, I., & O'Connell, M. E. (2021). Older adults' experiences with using technology for socialization during the COVID-19 pandemic. JMIR Aging, 4(2), e28010. https://doi.org/10.2196/28010

Haleem, A., Javaid, M., Qadri, M. A., & Suman, R. (2022). Understanding the role of digital technologies in education: A review. Sustainable Operations and Computers, 3, 275–285.

Hamari, J., Shernoff, D. J., Rowe, E., Coller, B., Asbell-Clarke, J., & Edwards, T. (2016). Challenging games help students learn: An empirical study on engagement, flow, and immersion in game-based learning. Computers in Human Behavior, 54, 170–179. https://doi.org/10.1016/j.chb.2015.07.045

Han, Z. (2024). ChatGPT in and for second language acquisition: A call for systematic research. Studies in Second Language Acquisition, 46(2), 301–306. https://doi.org/10.1017/S0272263124000111

Hasanein, A. M., & Sobaih, A. E. E. (2023). ChatGPT in higher education: Blessing or curse? Education and Information Technologies, 29, 1–21. https://doi.org/10.22521/edupij.2024.132.7

He, S. (2022). Review of Digital games and language learning: Theory, development and implementation. Language Learning & Technology, 26(1), 1–4.

HelloCappuccino. (2024). 6 ways to use Microsoft Copilot for language learning & practice. Retrieved from https://hellocappuccino.net/microsoft-copilot-for-language-learning/

Hossain, M. K., & Al Younus, M. A. (2024). Kahoot in the Classroom: A Game-Changer for Motivating English Grammar Learning in Tertiary Education in Bangladesh. Journal of Critical Studies in Language and Literature, 5(1), 24–31.

Hossain, M. K., & Al Younus, M. A. (2025). Teachers' perspectives on integrating ChatGPT into EFL writing instruction. TESOL Communications, 4(1), 41–60. https://doi.org/10.58304/tc.20250103

Hu, M., & Yuan, B. (2025). Innovations in language teaching methods based on multiple intelligences theory. International Journal of Educational Curriculum Management and Research, 6(1), 47–57. https://doi.org/10.38007/IJECMR.2025.060106

Huang, S., Willson, V., & Eslami, Z. (2012). The effects of task involvement load on L2 Incidental vocabulary learning: A meta-analytic study. The Modern Language Journal, 96(4), 544–557. https://doi.org/10.1111/j.1540-4781.2012.01394.x

Iglesias-Diéguez, K., Martínez-Adrián, M., & Gallardo-del-Puerto, F. (2025). Peer-to-peer interaction in task-based learning and the development of young EFL learners' productive vocabulary: an exploratory study. Language Awareness, 1–26. https://doi.org/10.1080/09658416.2025.2456754

Ishaq, K., Rosdi, F., Zin, N. A. M., Arshad, M. Y., & Ramadhani, A. (2022). Serious game design model for language learning in the cultural context. Educ Inf Technol, 27, 9317–9355. https://doi.org/10.1007/s10639-022-10999-5

Iskakova, M. (2024). Prospects for Using E-Learning Tools to Implement the Concept of "Lifelong Learning". E-Learning Innovations Journal, 2(2), 80–101. https://doi.org/10.57125/ELIJ.2024.09.25.05

Jain, S., Grewal, H., Vishnoi, A., Saxena, A., Bhardwaj, S., & Singh, R. (2025). Transformative trends: The impact of artificial intelligence (AI) on modern education. AIP Conference Proceedings, 3224(1), 020041. https://doi.org/10.1063/5.0246499

Javvaji, V. R., & Veera Raghavulu, P. (2025). The transformative impact of artificial intelligence on education. International Journal for Multidisciplinary Research (IJFMR). Retrieved from http://www.ijfmr.com

Jia, F., Sun, D., Ma, Q., & Looi, C. K. (2022). Developing an AI-based learning system for L2 learners' authentic and ubiquitous learning in English language. Sustainability, 14(23), 15527. https://doi.org/10.3390/su142315527

Jiang, P., Namaziandost, E., Azizi, Z., & Razmi, M. H. (2022). Exploring the effects of online learning on EFL learners' motivation, anxiety, and attitudes during the COVID-19 pandemic: a focus on Iran. Current Psychology. https://doi.org/10.1007/s12144-022-04013-x.

Jiang, R. (2022). How does artificial intelligence empower EFL teaching and learning nowadays? A review on artificial intelligence in the EFL context. Frontiers in Psychology, 13, 1049401. https://doi.org/10.3389/fpsyg.2022.1049401

Johnson, M., & Wang, T. (2024). Ethical concerns in AI-generated knowledge retrieval: Privacy, bias, and source reliability. International Journal of AI Ethics, 8(2), 102–118. https://doi.org/10.5678/ijaie.v8i2.3456

Johnston, L., Hassan, R., & Salih, A. (2024). Student perceptions of generative AI in higher education. Journal of Educational Technology & Society.

Johnston, R., Mark, R., & Masiello, I. (2024). Student perspectives on using ChatGPT in academic settings: A UK-based study. British Journal of Educational Technology, 55(2), 425–444.

Joshi, M. A. (2024). Adaptive learning through artificial intelligence. International Journal on Integrated Education, 7(2), 41–43. https://doi.org/10.2139/ssrn.4514887

Julian, A. S. (2022). The influence of PUBG Mobile online game on English learning. English Language Study and Teaching Journal (ELASTE), 3(2), 31–40. https://doi.org/10.2746-380X

Juris, J. J., Bouldin, E. D., Uva, K., Cardwell, C. D., Schulhoff, A., & Hiegl, N. (2022). Virtual intergenerational reverse-mentoring program reduces loneliness among older adults: Results from a pilot evaluation. International Journal of Environmental Research and Public Health, 19(12), 7121. https://doi.org/10.3390/ijerph19127121

Kapp, K. M. (2012). The gamification of learning and instruction: Game-based methods and strategies for training and education. Wiley.

Kara, N. (2021). A systematic review of the use of serious games in science education. Contemporary Educational Technology, 13(2), ep295. https://doi.org/10.30935/cedtech/9608

Karasimos, A. (2022). The battle of language learning apps: A cross-platform overview. Research Papers in Language Teaching and Learning, 12(1), 150–166.

Kavadella, A., Triantafyllopoulos, I., Kouskoura, S., & Laskaris, G. (2024). The impact of ChatGPT on student performance in dentistry education. Journal of Dental Education, forthcoming.

Kazu, İ. Y., & Kuvvetli, M. (2025). Digital language learning with Duolingo: assessing its impact on listening, speaking, reading, and writing skills. J. Comput. Educ. https://doi.org/10.1007/s40692-025-00355-0

Kelly, R. (2025). 2025 predictions: AI's impact on education. THE Journal. Retrieved from https://thejournal.com/Articles/2025/01/23/2025-Predictions-AIs-Impact-on-Education.aspx

Khattib, H., & Alt, D. (2024). A quasi-experimental study on the advantages of digital gamification using CoSpaces Edu application in science education. Educ Inf Technol, 29, 19963–19986. https://doi.org/10.1007/s10639-024-12635-w

Kim, J., Detrick, R., Yu, S., & Bae, S. (2025). Socially shared regulation of learning and artificial intelligence: Opportunities to support socially shared regulation. Educ Inf Technol. https://doi.org/10.1007/s10639-024-13187-9

Kim, Y. J., & Ifenthaler, D. (2019). Game-Based Assessment: The Past Ten Years and Moving Forward. In D. Ifenthaler & Y. J. Kim (Eds.), Game-Based Assessment Revisited. Advances in Game-Based Learning. Springer, Cham. https://doi.org/10.1007/978-3-030-15569-8_1

Kirginas, S. (2023). User Experience Evaluation Methods for Games in Serious Contexts. In K. M. L. Cooper & A. Bucchiarone (Eds.), Software Engineering for Games in Serious Contexts. Springer, Cham. https://doi.org/10.1007/978-3-031-33338-5_2

Klayklung, P., Chocksathaporn, P., Limna, P., Kraiwanit, T., & Jangjarat, K. (2023). Revolutionizing education with ChatGPT: Enhancing learning through conversational AI. Universal Journal of Educational Research, 2(3), 217–225. Retrieved from SSRN.

Klimova, B. (2020). Benefits of the use of mobile applications for learning a foreign language by elderly population. Procedia Computer Science, 176, 2184–2191. https://doi.org/10.1016/j.procs.2020.09.255

Klimova, B. (2021). Are there any cognitive benefits of computer-based foreign language training for healthy elderly people? – A mini-review. Frontiers in Psychology, 11, 573287.

Klimova, B., & Al-Obaydi, L. H. (2023). Use of mobile applications for foreign language learning among university students: needs and functions. International Journal of Interactive Mobile Technologies, 17(12), 28–39. https://doi.org/10.3991/ijim.v17i12.38541

Klimova, B., & Kacetl, J. (2017). Efficacy of computer games on language learning. TOJET, 16(4), 19–26.

Klimova, B., & Pikhart, M. (2020). Current research on the impact of foreign language learning among healthy seniors on their cognitive functions from a positive psychology perspective - A systematic review. Frontiers in Psychology, 11, 765. https://doi.org/10.3389/fpsyg.2020.00765

Klimova, B., & Pikhart, M. (2022). Application of corrective feedback using emerging technologies among L2 university students. Cogent Education, 9(1), 1–15.

Klimova, B., & Pikhart, M. (2025). Exploring the effects of artificial intelligence on student and academic well-being in higher education: A mini-review. Frontiers in Psychology, 16, 1498132. https://doi.org/10.3389/fpsyg.2025.1498132

Klimova, B., & Sanda, L. (2021). A novel educational smartphone application for cognitively healthy seniors: A pilot study. International Journal of Environmental Research and Public Health, 18(12), 6601. https://doi.org/10.3390/ijerph18126601

Klimova, B., Pikhart, M., & Al-Obaydi, L. (2024). The use of ChatGPT for academic writing in the university classroom: An exploratory study. Education and Information Technologies, Advance Online Publication.

Klimova, B., Pikhart, M., & Al-Obaydi, L. H. (2024). Exploring the potential of ChatGPT for foreign language education at the university level. Front. Psychol., 15, 1269319. https://doi.org/10.3389/fpsyg.2024.1269319

Klimova, B., Pikhart, M., & Kacetl, J. (2023). Ethical issues of the use of AI-driven mobile apps for education. Frontiers in Public Health, 10, 1118116. https://doi.org/10.3389/fpubh.2022.1118116

Klimova, B., Pikhart, M., Poláková, P., Cerna, M., Yayilgan, S. Y., & Shaikh, S. (2023). A systematic review on the use of emerging technologies in teaching English as an applied language at the university level. Systems, 11(1), 42. https://doi.org/10.3390/systems11010042

Kneer, J., Rieger, D., Ivory, J. D., & Ferguson, C. (2014). Awareness of risk factors for digital game addiction: Interviewing players and counselors. International Journal of Mental Health and Addiction, 12(4), 585–599.

Kohnke, L., Moorhouse, B. L., & Zou, D. (2023). ChatGPT for Language Teaching and Learning. RELC Journal, 1–14. https://doi.org/10.1177/00336882231162868

Krystalli, P., & Arvanitis, P. (2024). Serious games and gamification in foreign language learning: Trends and challenges (2015–2024) analyzed through text analysis techniques. European Journal of Education, 7(2). Aristotle University of Thessaloniki, Greece.

Lai, J. W. M., De Nobile, J., Bower, M., & Tan, E. (2022). Comprehensive evaluation of the use of technology in education – validation with a cohort of global open online learners. Educ Inf Technol, 27, 9877–9911. https://doi.org/10.1007/s10639-022-10986-w

Lampropoulos, G., & Sidiropoulos, A. (2024). Impact of Gamification on Students' Learning Outcomes and Academic Performance: A Longitudinal Study Comparing Online, Traditional, and Gamified Learning. Education Sciences, 14(4), 367. https://doi.org/10.3390/educsci14040367

Lasmawan, I. W., & Budiarta, I. W. (2020). Vygotsky's Zone of Proximal Development and the students' progress in learning (A heutagogical bibliographical review). Jurnal Pendidikan Indonesia (JPI), 9(4), 545–552. https://doi.org/10.23887/jpi-undiksha.v9i4.29915

Law, E. L. C., Kickmeier-Rust, M. D., Albert, D., & Holzinger, A. (2008). Challenges in the Development and Evaluation of Immersive Digital Educational Games. In A. Holzinger (Ed.), HCI and Usability for Education and Work. USAB 2008. Lecture Notes in Computer Science, 5298. Springer, Berlin, Heidelberg. https://doi.org/10.1007/978-3-540-89350-9_2

Leblebici, D. (2024). "You are Apple, why are you speaking to me in Turkish?": the role of English in voice assistant interactions. Multilingua, 43(4), 455–485. https://doi.org/10.1515/multi-2023-0072

Lee, S., Park, J., & Kim, M. (2024). Faculty preparedness and attitudes toward GenAI integration in higher education: A multi-institutional study. International Journal of Educational Technology in Higher Education, 21(1), 55.

Lei, A. (2025). Grok data analysis in Excel: A comprehensive guide. BytePlus. Retrieved from BytePlus, https://www.byteplus.com/en/topic/499486

Li, Y., Chen, D., & Deng, X. (2024). The impact of digital educational games on student's motivation for learning: The mediating effect of learning engagement and the moderating effect of the digital environment. PLoS ONE, 19(1), e0294350. https://doi.org/10.1371/journal.pone.0294350

Li, Z., & Li, J. (2022). Using the flipped classroom to promote learner engagement for the sustainable development of language skills: A mixed-methods study. Sustainability, 14(10), 5983.

Liao, S., Kruger, J., & Doherty, S. (2020). The impact of monolingual and bilingual subtitles on visual attention, cognitive load, and comprehension. The Journal of Specialised Translation, 33, 70–98.

Liu, F., Vadivel, B., Rezvani, E., & Namaziandost, E. (2021). Using games to promote English as a foreign language learners' willingness to communicate: Potential effects and teachers' attitude in focus. Frontiers in Psychology, 12, 1–10. https://doi.org/10.3389/fpsyg.2021.762447

Liu, J., & Shadiev, R. (2025). A review of empirical research on game-based digital citizenship education. Educ Inf Technol. https://doi.org/10.1007/s10639-025-13549-x

Loughton, M. (2025). PUBG popularity boosts language learning in digital games study. The Financial Analyst. Retrieved from https://thefinancialanalyst.net/2025/02/19/pubg-popularity-boosts-language-learning-in-digital-games-study/

Luckin, R. (2023). The ethical dimensions of AI in education: Balancing innovation with responsibility. International Journal of AI Ethics in Education, 9(2), 87–104. https://doi.org/10.1017/ijaie.2023.011

Lukov, T. S. (2022). Using Quizlet for academic vocabulary acquisition. TESOL Working Paper Series, 20, 34–52. http://www.hpu.edu

Macinska, S., & Vinkler, A. (2024). The role of AI in language learning: Research evidence and strategies for success. Cambridge Papers in English Language Education. Retrieved from https://www.cambridge.org/sites/default/files/media/documents/The_Role_of_AI_in_Language_Learning_Research_Evidence_and_Strategies.pdf

Mahapatra, S. (2024). Impact of ChatGPT on ESL students' academic writing skills: a mixed methods intervention study. Smart Learning Environments, 11(1), 9–18. https://doi.org/10.1186/s40561-024-00295-9

Majeed, A., Mudhsh, B. A., Bin-Hady, W. R. A., & Al-Tamimi, A. S. (2025). DeepSeek and Grok in the spotlight after ChatGPT in English education: A review study. Journal of English Studies in Arabia Felix, 4(1), 13–22. https://doi.org/10.56540/jesaf.v4i1.114

Mangen, A., Anda, L. G., Oxborough, G. H., & Brřnnick, K. (2015). Handwriting versus keyboard writing: Effect on word recall. Journal of Writing Research, 7(2), 227–247. https://doi.org/10.17239/jowr-2015.07.02.1

Marjanović, S. V., Patel, A., Adlakha, V., Aghajohari, M., BehnamGhader, P., Bhatia, M., Khandelwal, A., Kraft, A., Krojer, B., Lù, X. H., Meade, N., Shin, D., Kazemnejad, A., Kamath, G., Mosbach, M., Stańczak, K., & Reddy, S. (2025). DeepSeek-R1 Thoughtology: Let's <think> about LLM reasoning. arXiv preprint. https://doi.org/10.48550/arXiv.2504.07128

Marklund, B. B., & Alklind Taylor, A. S. (2016). Educational Games in Practice: The challenges involved in conducting a game-based curriculum. The Electronic Journal of e-Learning, 14(2), 122–121. www.ejel.org

Matić, L. J., & Abrantes Garcêz Palha, S. (2023). Integrating digital games in the classroom: a case study with game Probchallenge. Paper presented at 16th International Conference on Technology in Mathematics Teaching (ICTMT 16), Athene, Greece.

Mayer, R. E. (2019). Computer games for learning: An evidence-based approach. American Psychological Association. https://doi.org/10.1037/0000187-000

Meltzer, J. A., Kates Rose, M., Le, A. Y., Spencer, K. A., Goldstein, L., Gubanova, A., O'Connell, L. T., Breen, K., & Bialystok, E. (2021). Improvement in executive function for older adults through smartphone apps: A randomized clinical trial comparing language learning and brain training. Aging, Neuropsychology, and Cognition, 1–22. https://doi.org/10.1080/13825585.2021.1991262

Mengorio, T. M., & Dumlao, R. (2019). The Effect of Integrating Mobile Application in Language Learning: An Experimental Study. Journal of English Teaching, 5(1).

Mitsea, E., Drigas, A., & Skianis, C. (2025). A Systematic Review of Serious Games in the Era of Artificial Intelligence, Immersive Technologies, the Metaverse, an Neurotechnologies: Transformation Through Meta-Skills Training. Electronics, 14(4), 649. https://doi.org/10.3390/electronics14040649

Mogavi, R. H., Deng, C., Kim, J. J., Zhou, P., Kwon, Y. D., Metwally, A. H. S., Tlili, A., Bassanelli, S., Bucchiarone, A., Gujar, S., Nacke, L. E., & Hui, P. (2024). ChatGPT in education: A blessing or a curse? A qualitative study exploring early adopters' utilization and perceptions. Computers in Human Behavior: Artificial Humans, 2, 100027. https://doi.org/10.1016/j.chbah.2023.100027

Mohammed, S. J., & Khalid, M. W. (2025). Under the world of AI-generated feedback on writing: Mirroring motivation, foreign language peace of mind, trait emotional intelligence, and writing development. Language Testing in Asia, 15(7). https://doi.org/10.1186/s40468-025-00343-2

Naamati-Schneider, L., & Alt, D. (2024). Beyond digital literacy: The era of AI-powered assistants and evolving user skills. Education and Information Technologies, 29, 21263–21293. https://doi.org/10.1007/s10639-024-12694-z

Narushima, M., Liu, J., & Diestelkamp, N. (2018). Lifelong learning in active ageing discourse: its conserving effect on wellbeing, health and vulnerability. Ageing and Society, 38(4), 651–675. https://doi.org/10.1017/S0144686X16001136

Nasution, A. K. P. (2022). Social media used in language learning: Benefits and challenges. Journal of Linguistics, Literature and Language Teaching, 1(2), 59–68. https://jurnal-assalam.org/index.php/JLLLT/article/view/98

Natucci, G. C., & Borges, M. A. F. (2023). Balancing Game Elements, Learning, and Emotions in Game Design. In R. P. D. Santos & M. D. S. Hounsell (Eds.), Grand Research Challenges in Games and Entertainment Computing in Brazil - GranDGamesBR 2020–2030. Communications in Computer and Information Science, 1702. Springer, Cham. https://doi.org/10.1007/978-3-031-27639-2_5

Némethová, I. (2020). Autonomy and motivation in language learning and teaching. CASALC Review, 2020(1), 150–162. https://doi.org/10.5817/CASALC2020-1-12

Ng, D. T. K., Leung, J. K. L., Su, J., & Lo, M. K. Y. (2023). Teachers' AI digital competencies and twenty-first century skills in the post-pandemic world. Education Tech Research Dev, 71, 137–161. https://doi.org/10.1007/s11423-023-10203-6

Nguyen, T. N. T., Lai, N. V., & Nguyen, Q. T. (2024). Artificial Intelligence (AI) in education: A case study on ChatGPT's influence on student learning behaviors.

Nicolaidou, I., Pissas, P., & Boglou, D. (2021). Comparing immersive Virtual Reality to mobile applications in foreign language learning in higher education: a quasi-experiment. Interactive Learning Environments, 31(4), 2001–2015. https://doi.org/10.1080/10494820.2020.1870504

Nijmeijer, S. E., van Tol, M. J., Aleman, A., & Keijzer, M. (2021). Foreign language learning as cognitive training to prevent old age disorders? Protocol of a randomized controlled trial. Frontiers in Aging Neuroscience, 13, 550180. https://doi.org/10.3389/fnagi.2021.550180

Nilubol, K., & Sitthitikul, P. (2023). Gamification: Trends and opportunities in language teaching and learning practices. PASAA Journal, 67, 378–400.

Osman, N. I., & Abdul Rabu, S. N. (2020). Digital game-based language learning: A review of research trends on second language acquisition. ASM Science Journal, 13(Special Issue 3), 56–62. Centre for Instructional Technology and Multimedia, Universiti Sains Malaysia, Pulau Pinang, Malaysia.

Otero De Juan, N., & Garcia Laborda, J. (2012). Digital Games in Language Learning and Teaching (Book Review). In H. Reinders (Ed.), Digital Games in Language Learning and Teaching (256 pages). Palgrave Macmillan. ISBN: 1137022833 (pbk), 978-1137022837 (pbk).

Pan, F. (2024). AI in language teaching, learning, and assessment. IGI Global.

Panini, I. (2024). Microsoft Copilot AI: Complete guide and ready to use manual with integration in office 365. Amazon Digital Services LLC – Kdp.

Paoli, C. (2024). Microsoft Copilot gains actions feature, new agents in latest update. THE Journal. Retrieved from https://thejournal.com/Articles/2024/11/20/Microsoft-Copilot-Gains-Actions-Feature-New-Agents-in-Latest-Update.aspx

Park, J. (2022). Vocabulary learning through a daily task of cooking in the digital kitchen. Language Learning & Technology, 26(1), 1–22. https://hdl.handle.net/10125/73494

Patagar, M., Bulla, S., & Nayak, A. (2023). The digital divide: Access to technology and social inequality. International Journal of Research and Analytical Reviews, 10(1). Retrieved from IJRAR.

Pavlenko, A., & Syzenko, N. (2024). Academic integrity in the age of AI: Student and faculty perspectives. International Journal of Educational Integrity, forthcoming.

Perplexity AI. (2025). Concise and accurate knowledge retrieval using retrieval-augmented generation (RAG). Retrieved from https://perplexity.ai

Peterson, M., & Jabbari, N. (2023). Digital games in language learning: Case studies and applications. Oxon, New York: Routledge.

Peterson, M. (2010). Massively multiplayer online role-playing games as arenas for second language learning. Computer Assisted Language Learning, 23(5), 429–447. https://doi.org/10.1080/09588221.2010.520673

Pihlainen, K., Ehlers, A., Rohner, R., Cerna, K., Kärnä, E., Hess, M., Plettenberg, L., & Müller, C. (2022). Older adults' reasons to participate in digital skills learning: An interdisciplinary, multiple case study from Austria, Finland, and Germany. Studies in the Education of Adults, 55(1), 101–119. https://doi.org/10.1080/02660830.2022.2133268

Pikhart, M., & Al-Obaydi, L. H. (2023). Potential pitfalls of online foreign language teaching from the perspective of the university teachers. Heliyon, 9(1), e13732. https://doi.org/10.1016/j.heliyon.2023.e13732

Pikhart, M., & Al-Obaydi, L. H. (2025). Reporting the potential risk of using AI in higher education: Subjective perspectives of educators. Computers in Human Behavior Reports, 7(2), 45–62. https://doi.org/10.1016/j.chbr.2025.100693

Pikhart, M., Al-Obaydi, L. H., Klimova, B., & Tawafak, R. M. (2024b). The Impact of Digital Games on Motivation and Attitudes of EFL College Students. The Journal of Asia TEFL, 21(1). http://dx.doi.org/10.18823/asiatefl.2024.21.1.16.235

Pikhart, M., Klimova, B., & Al-Obaydi, L. H. (2024). Exploring university students' preferences and satisfaction in utilizing digital tools for foreign language learning. Frontiers in Education, 9. https://doi.org/10.3389/feduc.2024.1412377

Pikhart, M., Klimova, B., & Ruschel, F. B. (2023). Foreign language vocabulary acquisition and retention in print text vs. digital media environments. Systems, 11(1), 30. http://dx.doi.org/10.3390/systems11010030

Pikhart, M., Klimova, B., Al-Obaydi, L. H., Dziuba, S., & Cierniak-Emerych, A. (2022). The quantitative evaluation of subjective satisfaction with digital media in L2 acquisition in younger adults: A study from Europe, Asia, and Latin America. Frontiers in Psychology, 13, 1–8. https://doi.org/10.3389/fpsyg.2022.946187

Plass, J. L., Homer, B. D., & Kinzer, C. K. (2015). Foundations of game-based learning. Educational Psychologist, 50(4), 258–283. https://doi.org/10.1080/00461520.2015.1122533

Platzer, H. (2020). The role of Quizlet in vocabulary acquisition. Electronic Journal of Foreign Language Teaching, 17(2), 421–438.

Poláková, P., & Klímová, B. (2022). Vocabulary mobile learning application in blended English language learning. Frontiers in Psychology, 13, 869055. https://doi.org/10.3389/fpsyg.2022.869055

Prensky, M. (2001). Digital natives, digital immigrants Part 1. On the Horizon, 9(5), 1–6. https://doi.org/10.1108/10748120110424816

Puebla, C., Fievet, T., García, J., Tsopanidi, M., & Clahsen, H. (2022). Promoting social and collaborative language learning among older adults in the digital era: Development and evaluation of a smartphone app prototype. Gerontechnology, 21(1), 1–12. https://doi.org/10.4017/gt.2022.21.1.483.06

Puebla, C., Fievet, T., Tsopanidi, M., & Clahsen, H. (2021). Mobile-assisted language learning in older adults: Chances and challenges. ReCALL, 34(2), 169–184. https://doi.org/10.1017/S0958344021000276

Rahman, A., Mahir, S. H., Tashrif, M. T. A., Aishi, A. A., Karim, M. A., Kundu, D., Debnath, T., Moududi, M. A. A., & Eidmum, M. Z. (2025). Comparative analysis based on DeepSeek, ChatGPT, and Google Gemini: Features, techniques, performance, future prospects. arXiv preprint. https://doi.org/10.48550/arXiv.2503.04783

Ratnasari, W., Chou, T.-C., & Huang, C.-H. (2023). Exploring the Research Trajectory of Digital Game-based Learning: A Citation Network Analysis. Educational Technology & Society, 26(1), 45–61. [suspicious link removed]

Reinders, H., & Wattana, S. (2015). Can digital games facilitate language learning? ELT Journal, 69(3), 249–261. https://doi.org/10.1093/elt/ccv010

Reinhardt, J. (2019). Gameful second and foreign language teaching and learning: Theory, research, and practice. Palgrave Macmillan. https://doi.org/10.1007/978-3-030-04729-0

Reinhardt, J., & Thorne, S. (2020). "Digital games as language learning environments". In J. Plass, R. Mayer, & B. Homer (Eds.), Handbook of Game-based Learning, 409–436. Cambridge: MIT Press.

Reinhardt, J., & Sykes, J. (2012). Conceptualizing digital game-mediated L2 learning and pedagogy: Game-enhanced and game-based research and practice. In H. Reinders (Ed.), Digital games in language learning and teaching (pp. 32–49). Palgrave Macmillan.

Reinhardt, J., & Sykes, J. M. (2014). Special Issue Commentary: Digital Game Activity in L2 Teaching and Learning. Language Learning & Technology, 18(2), 2–8. http://llt.msu.edu/issues/june2014/commentary.pdf

Reiss, M. J. (2021). The use of AI in education: Practicalities and ethical considerations. London Review of Education, 19(1), 5.

Rossettini, G., Rodeghiero, L., Corradi, F., & Furlan, C. (2024). Comparative accuracy of ChatGPT-4, Microsoft Copilot and Google Gemini in the Italian entrance test for healthcare sciences degrees: a cross-sectional study. BMC Med Educ, 24, 694. https://doi.org/10.1186/s12909-024-05630-9

Roussel, S., & Galan, J.-P. (2018). Can clicker use support learning in a dual-focused second language German course? Language Learning & Technology, 22(3), 45–64. https://doi.org/10.125/44656

Saarinen, A., Lipsanen, J., Hintsanen, M., Huotilainen, M., & Keltikangas-Järvinen, L. (2021). The use of digital technologies at school and cognitive learning outcomes: A population-based study in Finland. International Journal of Educational Psychology, 10(1), 1–26. https://doi.org/10.17583/ijep.2021.4667

Şahin Kızıl, A., Klimova, B., Pikhart, M., & Parmaxi, A. (2025). A systematic review of the recent research on the usefulness of chatbots for language education. J Comput Assist Learn, 41, e70001. https://doi.org/10.1111/jcal.70001

Sanda, L., & Klimova, B. (2021). Educational mobile applications for learning English as a second language by Czech seniors. Procedia Computer Science, 192, 1848–1855.

Schiller, E., Dorner, H., & Szabó, Z. A. (2023). Developing older adults' learner autonomy through one-to-one counselling: Results of an exploratory investigation. System, 115, 103030. https://doi.org/10.1016/j.system.2023.103030

Sen, K., Prybutok, G., & Prybutok, V. (2022). The use of digital technology for social wellbeing reduces social isolation in older adults: A systematic review. SSM - Population Health, 17, 101020. https://doi.org/10.1016/j.ssmph.2021.101020

Shafiee Rad, H., Roohani, A., & Rahimi Domakani, M. (2021). Flipping EFL learners' writing classroom through role-reversal and discussion-oriented models. Language Learning & Technology, 25(2), 158–177. http://hdl.handle.net/10125/73438

Shandilya, E., & Fan, M. (2022). Understanding older adults' perceptions and challenges in using AI-enabled everyday technologies. arXiv preprint. https://arxiv.org/abs/2210.01369

Shute, V., Ke, F., & Wang, L. (2017). Assessment and adaptation in games. In P. Wouters & H. van Oostendorp (Eds.), Instructional Techniques to Facilitate Learning and Motivation of Serious Games. Advances in Game-Based Learning. Springer, Cham. https://doi.org/10.3319/39298-1_4

Silva, M., Mourão, E., Paiva, M. M., Viterbo, J., & Salgado, L. (2023). Privacy perceptions in digital games: A study with IT undergraduates. Lecture Notes in Computer Science, 14316, 183–194.

Singh, J., Tayarani-Najaran, M. H., & Yaqoob, I. (2023). The use of ChatGPT among university students: Perspectives on programming education. IEEE Access, 11, 11720–11735.

Singh, S., Tayarani-Najaran, M. H., & Yaqoob, I. (2023). ChatGPT in higher education: Opportunities and concerns from computer science students. Education and Information Technologies, forthcoming.

Şişianu, A., & Puşcaşu, A. (2024). New technologies and foreign language learning: Transforming language education. Journal of Social Sciences, 7(1), 91–99. https://doi.org/10.52326/jss.utm.2024.7(1).07

Sixsmith, A., Horst, B. R., Simeonov, D., & Mihailidis, A. (2022). Older people's use of digital technology during the COVID-19 pandemic. Bulletin of Science, Technology & Society, 42(1–2), 19–24. https://doi.org/10.1177/02704676221094731

SlideShare. (n.d.). A lesson plan on listening skills. Retrieved from https://www.slideshare.net/slideshow/sample-grade-10-apa-bibliography-detailed-lesson-plan/83831635

Smith, J., & Lee, R. (2025). AI-driven search engines: Enhancing information retrieval and accuracy. Journal of Artificial Intelligence and Data Science, 12(3), 155–172. https://doi.org/10.1234/jaids.v12i3.5678

Son, J.-B., Ružić, N. K., & Philpott, A. (2023). Artificial intelligence technologies and applications for language learning and teaching. Journal of China Computer-Assisted Language Learning, 12(3), 155–172. https://doi.org/10.1515/jccall-2023-0015

Sophonhiranrak, S. (2021). Features, barriers, and influencing factors of mobile learning in higher education: A systematic review. Heliyon, 7(4). https://doi.org/10.1016/j.heliyon.2021.e06696

Soroya, S. H., Al-Obaydi, L. H., & Rehman, M. A. (2023). Digital immigrants' attitudes toward e reading in Iraq and Pakistan. The Electronic Library, 41(4), 349–366. https://doi.org/10.1108/EL-09-2022-0217

Soyoof, A., Barry Lee Reynolds, Boris Vazquez-Calvo, & Katherine McLay. (2021). Informal digital learning of English (IDLE): a scoping review of what has been done and a look towards what is to come. Computer Assisted Language Learning. https://doi.org/10.1080/09588221.2021.1936562

Soyoof, A., Reynolds, B. L., Chan, K. K., Tseng, W. T., & McLay, K. (2023). Massive online multiplayer games as an environment for English learning among Iranian EFL students. Computer Assisted Language Learning, 1–44. https://doi.org/10.1080/09588221.2023.2171065

Sparks, J. R., Ober, T. M., Tenison, C., Arslan, B., Roll, I., Deane, P., Rivera, D. Z., Gooch, R. M., & O'Reilly, T. (2024). Opportunities and challenges for assessing digital and AI literacies. ETS Research Report. https://www.ets.org/pdfs/rd/ets-digital-literacy-ai-full-report.pdf

Stockwell, G. (2013). Technology and motivation in English-language teaching and learning. In E. Ushioda (Ed.), International Perspectives on Motivation. International Perspectives on English Language Teaching. Palgrave Macmillan, London. https://doi.org/10.1057/9781137000873_9

Su, F., & Zou, D. (2020). Technology-enhanced collaborative language learning: theoretical foundations, technologies, and implications. Computer Assisted Language Learning, 35(8), 1754–1788. https://doi.org/10.1080/09588221.2020.1831545

Suman, C., & Suman, S. (2023). Using artificial intelligence for foreign language learning. Talent Publication, 1(1), 57–64. https://www.researchgate.net/publication/374119563

Sundqvist, P. (2019). Commercial-off-the-shelf games in the digital wild and L2 learner vocabulary. Language Learning & Technology, 23(1), 87–113. https://doi.org/10.125/44674

Tawafak, R. M., Al-Obaydi, L. H., & Pikhart, M. (2023). Competency categorization and roles of online teachers from the perspective of university students. Front. Psychol., 14, 1009000. https://doi.org/10.3389/fpsyg.2023.1009000

Tawafak, R. M., Al-Obaydi, L. H., Klimova, B., & Pikhart, M. (2023). Technology integration of using digital gameplay for enhancing EFL college students' behavior intention. Contemporary Educational Technology, 15(4), ep452. https://doi.org/10.30935/cedtech/13454

Tawafak, R. M., Al-Obaydi, L. H., Pikhart, M., & Namaziandost, E. (2024). Risk-taking, TAM model, and technology integration: Impact on EFL college students' behavioral intentions. Applied Research on English Language, 8(2), 140729. https://are.ui.ac.ir/article_28324.html

Tawafak, R. M., Al-Rahmi, W. M., Alshimai, A., Alyoussef, I. Y., & Aldaijy, A. (2025). Exploring the impact of digital gameplay on behavioral intentions in learning graphics programming courses. Contemporary Educational Technology, 17(2), ep576. https://doi.org/10.30935/cedtech/16115

Tawafak, R. M., Romli, A. B., bin Abdullah Arshah, R., & Almaroof, R. A. S. (2018). Assessing the impact of technology learning and assessment method on academic performance. EURASIA Journal of Mathematics, Science and Technology Education, 14(6), 2241–2254.

Teachflow.AI. (2022). AI in education: Global success stories unveiled. Teachflow.AI. Retrieved from Teachflow.AI. https://teachflow.ai/ai-in-education-global-success-stories-unveiled

Teng, M. F. (2021). Interactive-whiteboard-technology-supported collaborative writing: Writing achievement, metacognitive activities, and co-regulation patterns. System, 97, 102426. https://doi.org/10.1016/j.system.2020.102426

TESOL International Association. (n.d.). Lesson plan: Skills-based vocabulary teaching engagement activities. Retrieved from [suspicious link removed]

Thelwall, M. (2024). Can ChatGPT evaluate research quality? A pilot study using REF-like criteria. Journal of Informetrics, 18(1), 101480.

Thelwall, M. (2024). Evaluating ChatGPT for research support in academia. Journal of Documentation.

Thurairasu, V. (2022). Gamification-Based Learning as The Future of Language Learning: An Overview. European Journal of Humanities and Social Sciences, 2(6), 62–69. https://doi.org/10.24018/ejsocial.2022.2.6.353

Tiernan, P., Costello, E., Donlon, E., Parysz, M., & Scriney, M. (2023). Information and media literacy in the age of AI: Options for the future. Education Sciences, 13(9), 906. https://doi.org/10.3390/educsci13090906

Tiwari, H., Jain, S., Kumar, S., Soni, V., & Negi, A. (2024). AI-driven English language learning: Leveraging applications/APIs for dynamic content and feedback. World Journal of Advanced Research and Reviews, 22(3), 1611–1616. https://doi.org/10.30574/wjarr.2024.22.3.1882

Treve, M. (2025). Integrating artificial intelligence in education: Impacts on student learning and innovation. International Journal of Vocational Education and Training Research, 10(2), Article 14. https://doi.org/10.11648/j.ijvetr.20241002.14

Turow, J. (2025). DeepSeek's new model shows that AI expertise might matter more than compute in 2025. DeepSeek.

Umejima, K., Ibaraki, T., Yamazaki, T., & Sakai, K. L. (2021). Paper notebooks vs. mobile devices: Brain activation differences during memory retrieval. Frontiers in Behavioral Neuroscience, 15, 634158. https://doi.org/10.3389/fnbeh.2021.634158

Urlaub, P., & Dessein, E. (2022). Machine translation and foreign language education. Frontiers in Artificial Intelligence, 5, 936111. https://doi.org/10.3389/frai.2022.936111

Uus, Õ., Mettis, K., & Väljataga, T. (2022). Self-directed learning: A case-study of school students scientific knowledge construction outdoors. Cogent Education, 9(1). https://doi.org/10.1080/2331186X.2022.2074342

van der Ploeg, M., Keijzer, M., & Lowie, W. (2023). Language pedagogies and late-life language learning proficiency. International Review of Applied Linguistics in Language Teaching. https://doi.org/10.1515/iral-2023-0079

VanWinkle, J. (2024). AI in education: Transformative use cases, success stories, and challenges. Artificial Intelligence. Retrieved from Kubernet. https://www.kubernet.dev/ai-in-education-transformative-use-cases-success-stories-and-lessons-learned

Verma, N. (2023). How effective is AI in education? 10 case studies and examples. Axon Park. Retrieved from Axon Park.

Vieriu, A. M., & Petrea, G. (2025). The impact of Artificial Intelligence (AI) on students' academic development. Education Sciences, 15(3), 343. https://doi.org/10.3390/educsci15030343

Viktorova, L. V., Kocharian, A. B., & Korotun, O. O. (2018). Information and communication technologies in foreign language education for "third-age" learners. Information Technologies and Learning Tools, 63(1), 22.

Vnucko, G., & Klimova, B. (2023). Exploring the potential of digital game-based vocabulary learning: A systematic review. Systems, 11(2), 57.

Vu, P., & Feinstein, S. (2017). An exploratory multiple case study about using game-based learning in STEM classrooms. International Journal of Research in Education and Science (IJRES), 3(2), 582–588. https://doi.org/10.21890/ijres.328087

Vuorikari, R., Pokropek, A., & Muñoz, J. C. (2025). Enhancing digital skills assessment: introducing compact tools for measuring digital competence. Tech Know Learn. https://doi.org/10.1007/s10758-025-09825-x

Walter, Y. (2024). Embracing the future of Artificial Intelligence in the classroom: the relevance of AI literacy, prompt engineering, and critical thinking in modern education. Int J Educ Technol High Educ, 21, 15. https://doi.org/10.1186/s41239-024-00448-3

Wang, L. (2023). The impact of student-centered learning on academic motivation and achievement: A comparative research between traditional instruction and student-centered approach. Journal of Education, Humanities and Social Sciences, 22, 346–353. https://doi.org/10.54097/ehss.v22i.12463

Wang, X., & Johnson, D. (2025). AI-powered automated assessment and feedback: A future perspective on grading efficiency. Educational Technology Research and Development, 73(1), 45–66. https://doi.org/10.1186/s41239-025-00322-w

Wang, Y., & Christiansen, M. S. (2019). An investigation of Chinese older adults' self-directed English learning experience using mobile apps. International Journal of Computer-Assisted Language Learning and Teaching, 9(4), 51–71. https://doi.org/10.4018/IJCALLT.2019100104

Wangsa, K., Karim, S., Gide, E., & Elkhodr, M. (2024). A systematic review and comprehensive analysis of pioneering AI chatbot models from education to healthcare: ChatGPT, Bard, Llama, Ernie and Grok. Future Internet, 16(219). https://doi.org/10.3390/fi16070219

Wichadee, S., & Pattanapichet, F. (2018). Enhancement of performance and motivation through application of digital games in an English language class. Teaching English with Technology, 18(1), 77–92. http://www.tewtjournal.org

Williams, K. L. (2024). A first look at using Microsoft's new AI tool, Copilot. Journal of Accountancy. Retrieved from https://www.journalofaccountancy.com/issues/2024/mar/a-first-look-at-using-microsofts-new-ai-tool-copilot.html

Williams, K., & Roberts, S. (2024). Learn LM: Improving Gemini for Learning. arXiv preprint. Retrieved from https://arxiv.org/abs/2403.12345

Wu, L. (2025). Application of artificial intelligence in teaching English as a foreign language: Progress, challenges, and trends. English Language Teaching and Learning Studies, 6(4), 215–229. https://doi.org/10.22158/ELTLS.V6N4P215

Wulan, D. R., Nainggolan, D. M., Hidayat, Y., Rohman, T., & Fiyul, A. Y. (2024). Exploring the benefits and challenges of gamification in enhancing student learning outcomes. Global International Journal of Innovative Research, 2(7), 1657–1674. https://doi.org/10.59613/global.v2i7.238

Xiao, Y., Zhang, T., & He, J. (2024). The promises and challenges of AI-based chatbots in language education through the lens of learner emotions. Heliyon, 10(18), e37238. https://doi.org/10.1016/j.heliyon.2024.e37238

Xu, D., & Garcia, M. (2024). AI-driven tools for multilingual support and accessibility in education. Journal of Educational Innovation, 15(3), 102–120. https://doi.org/10.1007/s11625-024-00378-2

Xu, Z., Chen, Z., Eutsler, L., & Zheng, L. (2020). A scoping review of digital game-based technology on English language learning. Education Tech Research Dev, 68, 877–904. https://doi.org/10.1007/s11423-019-09702-2

Yanes, N., & Bououd, I. (2019). Using gamification and serious games for English language learning: Results from a Delphi study in the context of Jouf University. International Conference on Computer and Information Sciences (ICCIS). https://doi.org/10.1109/ICCISci.2019.8125

Yang, J., Yin, C. X., & Wang, W. (2018). Flipping the classroom in teaching Chinese as a foreign language. Language Learning & Technology, 22(1), 16–26. https://dx.doi.org/10.125/44575

Zamborová, K., Stefanutti, I., & Klimová, B. (2021). CercleS survey: impact of the COVID-19 pandemic on foreign language teaching in Higher education. Language Learning in Higher Education, 11(2), 269–283.

Zawacki-Richter, O., & Latchem, C. (2023). The future of AI in education: Ethical considerations and policy development. Education Policy Review, 21(4), 233–250. https://doi.org/10.1080/02680939.2023.1802545

Zdravkova, K. (2022). The potential of artificial intelligence for assistive technology in education. In M. Ivanović, A. Klašnja-Milićević, & L. C. Jain (Eds.), Handbook on Intelligent Techniques in the Educational Process. Learning and Analytics in Intelligent Systems, 29. Springer, Cham. https://doi.org/10.1007/978-3-031-04662-9_4

Zhai, C., Wibowo, S., & Li, L. D. (2024). The effects of over-reliance on AI dialogue systems on students' cognitive abilities: a systematic review. Smart Learn. Environ., 11, 28. https://doi.org/10.1186/s40561-024-00316-7

Zhang, C. (2021). The advantages and disadvantages of learning a second language early. Advances in Social Science, Education and Humanities Research, 631, 32–37.

Zhang, M. (2023). Older people's attitudes towards emerging technologies: A systematic literature review. Public Understanding of Science, 32(8), 948–968. https://doi.org/10.1177/09636625231171677

Zhao, X., Ren, Y., & Cheah, K. S. L. (2023). Leading virtual reality (VR) and augmented reality (AR) in education: Bibliometric and content analysis from the Web of Science (2018–2022). SAGE Open, 13(3), 1–23. https://doi.org/10.1177/21582440231190821

Zhu, D. (2012). Using games to improve students' communicative ability. Journal of Language Teaching and Research, 3(4), 801–805. https://doi.org/10.4304/jltr.3.4.801-805

Notes on the Authors

Blanka Klímová serves as the Vice-Dean for International Relations at the Faculty of Informatics and Management, University of Hradec Králové, Czech Republic. She is also a professor in the Department of Applied Linguistics. Her teaching and research focus primarily on English for Specific Purposes (ESP) and the integration of digital tools in foreign language education. In addition to her pedagogical work, she supervises doctoral students both domestically and internationally. Prof Klímová is an active member of multiple research councils and editorial boards and frequently contributes as a chair or member of conference committees at both national and international levels. With an extensive research portfolio, she has authored over 300 original and review articles indexed in Web of Science. Her leadership in academic projects includes, for example, serving as the head of a working group in the COST project (CA19102) – Language in the Human-Machine Era and as the project leader for the Grant of the Fund for Bilateral Relations (Reg. No. EHP-BFNU-OVNKM-4-257-01-2023) – Artificial Intelligence in Formal Foreign Language Education. Recognised for her scholarly contributions, she has been ranked among the World's Top 2% Scientists by Stanford University's Global List – three times for a single year (2020, 2022, 2024) and twice for her career-long impact (2020, 2024).

Marcel Pikhart is Head of the Centre for Basic and Applied Research and Associate Professor in the Department of Applied Linguistics at the Faculty of Informatics and Management at the University of Hradec Králové, Czech Republic. His research interests span various domains of linguistics, including psycholinguistics, cognitive linguistics, and applied linguistics. Specifically, he focuses on psycholinguistic aspects such as second language (L2) acquisition and the quality of life related to L2 acquisition in older adults. In cognitive linguistics, he explores intercultural categories and their interpretation. His work in applied linguistics encompasses L2 acquisition, English as a Second Language (ESL), and foreign language learning. He is also interested in the intersection of cognitive and technological aspects of communication, particularly in the context of human–computer interaction (HCI) and its implications for higher education. He has been recognised for his contributions to the field, including being listed in Stanford University's Global List of the World's Top 2% of Scientists in both 2022 and 2023. His academic output is extensive, comprising numerous publications in impact journals, books, and papers indexed in Scopus, SSCI, and ESCI, as well as conference proceedings listed in Scopus and Web of Science.

*

Liqaa Habeb Al-Obaydi is an Iraqi scholar specialising in English language teaching, applied linguistics, and educational technology. She is currently Professor in the English Department at the College of Education for Human Sciences, University of Diyala, Iraq. Al-Obaydi earned her Bachelor's degree in English Language from the University of Diyala in 2004, followed by a Master's degree in Methods of Teaching English as a Second or Foreign Language in 2007. She later obtained a PhD in Philosophy of Education and Psychology, focusing on Methods of Teaching English, from the University of Baghdad in 2014. Her research interests span English language teaching methodologies, human–computer interaction, psycholinguistics, and the integration of innovative technologies in education. She has presented her work at numerous national and international conferences, including events in Turkey, Malaysia, Dubai, Thailand, and Russia. She was honoured during the Iraqi Scientific Day 2024 awards ceremony. This prestigious event, hosted by the Ministry of Higher Education and Scientific Research, recognises outstanding contributions to scientific research, global publishing, and academic excellence in Iraq. Al-Obaydi has published extensively in high-impact, well-known academic journals, many of which are Scopus-indexed and ranked Q1 in their respective fields such as Interactive Learning Environments, Current Psychology, Heliyon, Education and Information Technologies, and many others. Her research covers language education, AI-driven learning, digital gaming, and cognitive engagement, making significant contributions to EFL teaching methodologies and educational technology.

Digital Learning and the Future

Edited by Kieran McCartney and Graeme Davis

This interdisciplinary book series examines the use of digital technology in education. It is part of an unfolding educational agenda around technology-enhanced learning, where technology is both blended as a tool within existing pedagogies and drives new pedagogies. The series looks to the future, to emerging technologies and methodologies. Areas of interest include educational futures and future pedagogies, pedagogy and globalization (including MOOC), mobile learning, edtech, technology in assessment, the use of AI in education, and technology and face-to-face blended learning.

The series encourages proposals for short-format books (between 25,000 and 50,000 words) with the aim of responding quickly to this rapidly changing field. Short monographs, co-authored or edited collections, case studies, practical guides and more are also all welcome.

Vol.1 Kieran McCartney

Personalised Learning and Assessment in Remote Education: A Guide for Educators and Learners. 166 Pages. 2021.

ISBN 9781789979459

Vol. 2 Blanka Klímová, Marcel Pikhart and Liqaa Habeb Al-Obaydi
Rethinking Language Education in the Digital Era. 144 pages. 2026.

ISBN 9781805842668

www.ingramcontent.com/pod-product-compliance
Ingram Content Group UK Ltd.
Pitfield, Milton Keynes, MK11 3LW, UK
UKHW020124290926
15471UKWH00003B/267

9 781805 842668